Ripples On A Global Pond

*Coping with Change when
You or Your Loved Ones Emigrate*

Christa F. de Vries

authorHOUSE®

AuthorHouse™ UK Ltd.
500 Avebury Boulevard
Central Milton Keynes, MK9 2BE
www.authorhouse.co.uk
Phone: 08001974150

First published by AuthorHouse   12/23/2010

ISBN: 978-1-4520-9383-3 (sc)

This book is printed on acid-free paper.

Contents

Introduction

Why talk about emigration and its challenges if you only want to have a quick look at the impact of moving abroad on you and your loved ones? Or if you only want confirmation for a decision almost or already made? Perhaps wanting to browse through someone else's experiences just to see what others say?

How serious are you about the real thing called 'emigration'? That it is a process and often, one far beyond expectation? Do you realize that transitional change in your personal life in a new country could become a real and unexpected turning point? Perhaps even an unwelcome one? Have you considered the emotional impact of moving to another country? Are you ready for it?

If you are, you may find that this part of your life's journey will lead you down routes you will eventually have mapped out for yourself, leaving behind your own Columbian cross. Not really a road constructed by others, or a route selected by unknown forces, but your own, chosen ways towards your destination, even if it does not feel like that.

Perhaps you do not view moving abroad as emigration, and have not thought about it as your life's journey – especially if you do not move too far away and maintain citizenship of your original country. Like 'only' moving across the English Channel, or relocating to sunny Spain or friendly Australia, not too far away from your original rainy address.

It may be that you think about emigration as an issue 'others' have –

those who move from East to West, North to South, and of migrant workers and illegal immigrants who overflow first world countries.

Perhaps you would like to think again as there are so much more to leaving your country to settle somewhere else (emigration); to the process of settling somewhere in another country (immigration) and even to moving between countries (migration). It is a process of change, mostly a lengthy one.

The process of change connected to emigration involves similar issues to any big change in your personal life. It reveals the common factors that are involved when people have to, or want to, make *that* big change in their personal lives. It is just that this time, the process could linger, unfold hidden motives, and could bring about hopeless endings - even endless hope.

You realize that change does not only occur when you move to another country, far away. It can happen anytime and anywhere. And if you think that this book will give you some quick advice on whether you should go or stay, or should make those changes, which you have postponed for so long, now, you will be disappointed.

The process of leaving a country, arriving in a new one, and adapting to new surroundings does not happen overnight. Deciding to leave your country is a decision that is not taken lightly. Entering the process of ongoing change as a consequence thereto is to expose your self to a process that cuts deeply into the real meaning of the concept of personal transitional change.

With the process of emigration, and settling in another country, change touches every part of your being – your conscience, emotions, dreams, spirituality, relationships, and hopes. In short: it touches everything.

Emigration is one of those things that involve everything that you would normally experience when you want to make a significant, far-reaching change in your life.

Perhaps it is because change is a consistent, continuous process that uses all of its tentacles to seek, find and absorb its subject. With its tentacles stretching and crawling into every part of your existence, you will slowly discover its slyness, ruthlessness and brilliance.

During this change there might be things underpinning your emotional experiences that you perhaps would prefer not to discuss or reveal - things that other immigrants also experienced, but would not tell you about. Just because these were so intensely personal, but then, if you would have consciously known and admitted these, perhaps your own decisions would have been different.

It is not always easy to recognize, or to admit, that below the surface of the conscious mind, there are lying things hidden that most of the time become the driving force behind your decisions and destination. They drive you towards your goal, or away from it. As much as they result in positive experiences, as much can the opposite be true. Like in the case of a big change made.

Change will sometimes gradually, and other times rapidly, give you moments of sudden reality, shock, or instant realization that there is no turning back. You move through these motions with their distinct characteristics and their, often, draining demands. Through some you move through smoothly, through others often zombie-like, stupefied and even impatiently. But, eventually, you will stand in awe, often victoriously looking back at yourself, at that someone you once knew, or thought you knew. And then, out of the blue may the realization strike you: the empowering feeling of having made it, of having arrived…

Although this book deals with the impact of change on people and their families resulting from emigration and settling in another country, it also applies to anyone who is undergoing any type of transitional change.

It deals with the psychological and socio-psychological aspects of change, as a process of transition, and with specific aspects of emigration and resettling, which are linked to the different phases of the cycle of change. I discuss ways to cope with these.

In short, the book deals with those things people (especially immigrants) would rather not talk about. Things they would not tell you voluntarily, even if you asked.

While planning this book, I initially thought of approaching the subject academically, keeping in mind that it is a process interwoven with strange discoveries and deep emotions. Emotions of the people I had arranged to interview, and also my own. However, after spending time with immigrants, I came to realize, more than ever, that transitional change in a person's life is never experienced fragmentally, or on the surface. It touches you in totality – mind, body and soul. It leaves its mark, sometimes a scar, and many times a point of growth.

Having interviewed many immigrants from countries across the globe, who were living in England at the time of my explorative research, and having talked to some Britons who have tried living abroad, I realize how much the emotional impact of emigration can influence and direct your future.

Unfortunately, not always in a positive way. It is therefore with awe and respect (how could I do this otherwise?) that I have been writing. I am filled with apprehension and hesitation about that which will inevitably become the journey to one's inner self – being an immigrant living abroad.

I sometimes wonder, where does the decision to undertake such a significant change start? Just to realize, all of a sudden, in that one Zen-moment, that it actually happened inside, perhaps a long time ago.

Change entails an element of ambition. This ambition would have been triggered by something happening during a significant point in your life. You may probably find that it comes down to a hidden desire for success, adventure or expansion, and a testing of your abilities. By recognizing this, and having the courage and the inner motivation, you will start to plan your first movements towards your unknown destination. Before you know it, you will be where I, and many others, am now.

At such a significant halt in one's own cycle of change, which also includes your current life cycle, at least you can say that you know why you are living – to persevere through depths of doubt, and often difficult times. Times that have forced you along life's pathways towards the eventual moment of feeling almost complete – by experiencing the wonder of spiritual awareness and the powerful healing that it brings.

At this stage, there will be several discoveries. The most obvious and enlightening one is realising your inner strength - and that you were created with much more than you are able to put into words. That you do not create this change, but rather, you allow change to ripple through your mind and body to create something special within you.

During this process, you may also discover what I, and others, have learnt along the way – that goals are changeable and adjustable, and that it is a goal in itself to be able to acknowledge and admit to something that you would not have done otherwise. Is it not true that positive change can only begin once a person admits the reality of his uncertain or crippling circumstances? Or when he admits to his own shortcomings? To vocalize that thing which is actually holding you back, like a chain on a convict's leg, hindering his escape?

The chain will hold you back, slow down your movement, and hurt your ankle. It will eventually tie you down, as your steps forward may become extremely difficult, perhaps impossible. But on the other hand, there are many for whom it has worked out well. What about you? Is that what you want, too?

Depending on how you approach it, transitional change in your personal life may become the miraculous medium through which you and your family learn to discover and realize the wonder of life. You will find new horizons, develop coping skills, and embark upon a new life – in the case of emigration, literally.

By looking deeper into the process of emigration rather than just thinking about it in terms of moving house and changing country, it

5

will expose those often terrifying underlying issues, which confront people during the different stages of their big change.

This book, therefore, is meant for everyone who has been confronted with the apprehension of forthcoming, unavoidable personal change. That scary decision which needs to be made, the unknown factors which lie ahead and the impact of sudden opportunities on the horizon.

It will be of meaning to anyone who is facing emigration, or who has connections with an immigrant, be it through work, at church, or in the social community. If you are in an authoritative post, or assigned a senior position to an immigrant, you will most likely want to learn how to understand these underlying issues. Thereby, you will also understand more of those factors underlying your own process of transitional change.

In the experiences of emigrants, migrants and immigrants, specifically in their emotions and the consequential challenges to deal with such enormous change, you may start to see yourself addressing those changes that you are being exposed to in your own personal life.

And when you realize that you are currently on the brink of your own big personal change, you may learn how to manage it effectively. This book will help you through this process if you allow yourself to develop new insights, test and try new skills, and accept that you are an evolving being, no matter what your age.

That is why I am addressing this book to both the emigrant and the immigrant, and also to you. Have these people embarked upon something which, in many respects, mirrors some of your own desires, thoughts, fears, hesitations, losses, and taking up new challenges?

Is it not that when you decide to make a significant change in your life, that you emigrate from the present you know, to an unknown future?

'Immigrant.' Is it a swear word? No, in this context it is just another word for 'having made the big change.' But before you make that decision to move abroad, think it through thoroughly.

Your new address is not only a telephone call away; it is also miles of emotional cycles away. Emotional miles, which will either stretch or shrink depending on how you deal with the issues involved.

PART 1:
The Challenges

Chapter 1
Contemplating moving
to another country

Perhaps you are the lucky one who wants to move to another country, and do not have to go against your will, or because you have been caught up in difficult circumstances. Perhaps you have been considering this move for a while now, and have already started emailing job agencies abroad.

Perhaps you are someone who has been offered a secure job in a new country, with the company's prospects and promises painted in gold. You know you want to, and can be, a success in the new world that lies abroad. On the other hand, perhaps sad, unsafe, and insecure circumstances make you feel that you have no other choice but to leave your beloved country. Or maybe you want to be closer to family who already live abroad, and whom you miss so much.

The fact is, you know you want to go, leaving behind everything you have worked for – a house, a secure job and established relationships. All that is left to be done is to tell family and friends about the decision and to pluck up the courage to do it.

So, why do you still ponder the thought? Why do you sometimes wake up in the night and realize that major decisions like these can never happen overnight, and that you need much more time to think? Do you start to wonder if your friend's opinion is really true, that there is too much at stake? Will the price you pay for this dream be too high?

For some it works out fine – for others, not. And what about you? How many things will turn out well for you and your family? What exactly do you need to consider before making one of the biggest, and perhaps most stressful, moves of your life? How much do you know about the process of change and transition, especially if this process comes knocking at your door?

And what if you have already been in the new country for quite a while now? What makes it work for you, and what doesn't?

Having gone through the process of emigration myself, and having learnt from many people all over the world who have undergone the same experience, I feel compelled to share those unspoken and often frightening issues, which underlie the process of emigration and settling into life in a new country.

I feel to share these, because I am concerned – concerned about people who seem to be missing the stepping-stones leading towards successful adjustment in a new country, and for those who have deeply regretted their decision to move abroad. Over years I have witnessed how much too many people have been affected by the consequences of their decision.

My wish for you is that this book will help you to make that life-changing decision, or a decision, which, eventually, you will recognize as having been the right one for you. I want to help you understand and deal with the issues and opportunities on the road that you will be traveling.

For in the end, it is you who will have to deal with the consequences – positive ones, and negative ones, depending on the choices you have made and are still making.

Although you cannot tell the future, you can at least prepare yourself for the unknown, because you will have to apply all your emotional, spiritual, and cognitive abilities in order to deal with what lies ahead – the road that you have chosen. It is by knowing this that you will be better prepared for dealing with the future.

For me, it started, as for so many others, during happy times back home. It was a time when I was living happily with my husband and our daughter in a beautiful, friendly and secure neighbourhood close to the best of amenities in Johannesburg, South Africa. We were living close to our friends, and not too far away from family.

Some of them lived one hour away by car, and others were two to three hours away. My husband's son and his family lived in the Stellenbosch area near Cape Town, about fourteen hours away by car, and a two-hour flight. Now that we live apart, it is between thirteen and twenty-three hours by plane, depending on availability and affordability of the flight.

We have all enjoyed wonderful times together, with exquisite family gatherings around the swimming pool under the hot South African sun, eating *braaivleis* (barbecue) and *potjiekos* (a stew-like dish, which is slow-cooked on the coals all day in a black, three-legged iron pot.)

Time after time, the hadedas, a brown and pink ibis, would suddenly squeal - a frightening, noisy sound - when they would fly from the *apiesdoring*-tree branch above our heads into the bluest, widest African sky.

And every time we laughed when my husband or brother-in-law told the same joke: 'Why do hadedas squeal when they fly off?' 'Why? someone would ask, loyally. 'Because they have a fear of heights...' And we would all laugh hysterically, as if hearing the joke for the first time.

Other times, we would just sit dreamily, quietly, with my parents on their front stoop, somewhere in the vast Free State, watching the African sun set red and amber over the distant hills.

That is what I call a loving family.

Never in my life did I imagine that the day would come to say goodbye to them all, to not go home until the next time, but to pull up my roots and move to England – lock, stock and barrel, with my husband and child.

As the decision was made after a lengthy period of consideration and evaluation, we had prepared everyone (or so I thought) and felt prepared enough ourselves, to wave a last goodbye from a distance behind the security doors at Departures, at Johannesburg International Airport. In our hands, we held one-way tickets to Heathrow, London.

Years later – it is now the first decade of the new millennium. In England, hot summer days are limited and British barbecues still involve mostly sausages and burgers. There are no hadedas, and the sky is not often wide and blue.

Friends have replaced family and when there is a rare opportunity for a family member to come and visit, you cherish every second, as if it were the last.

One day, on a previous visit home, someone remarked: 'She has changed.' For a moment, this comment shocked me and I had to ponder the thought. What impact would this change have on my relationships with people at home? Would they still love me as much as before, even though I was a 'changed person'? Did I really want to be a 'changed' person?

But we all change as time moves on, because change brings about change, whether you want it to or not. Change also brings about transition, a process, which happens inside you. But despite the change and transition, we know that our dear ones still love us, just as we still love them.

It is this process that I am writing about. Underlying my motivation is a curiosity about the thing that makes it work for some and not for others. Why is change a challenge and at the same time, a devastating experience, yet in another situation, it can become and stay the major attraction, which pulls you through?

I was astounded at the revelations of a large number of people living in London, who are immigrants from so many different countries. Some I met at church, others at work, or socially, or I assessed them professionally as part of my work. Others have passed me by on the streets, trains and buses.

All of us are the product of the same thing, and although we are strangers, we share a common factor – that of change and finding ourselves in the everlasting process of adjustment to the new. All of us are people who have gone through the challenging process of transitional change, with the common goal of creating a home away from home.

For some, the experience has been painful, in some ways even destructive, and for others, it has been a challenge with positive results. I would guess that for many people who look back on their life journey, the process will be an enriching experience and a learning curve, despite the ups and downs that are typical of the process of change and transition.

The reason? There appears to be something strong, determined and purposeful about many of those who have undertaken that giant step from a known comfort zone into the new and unknown world, those who have embraced the process of transitional change.

To really understand the essence of transitional change brought about by relocation to a new country, it is necessary to understand exactly what the change and transitions involve. Not only the physical changes but also the emotional, psychological, spiritual, social, occupational, and even neurological processes – those things that we do not always talk about.

All these elements play an active, interactive and crucial role in the process of change. It is vital to understand their effect on the person and the consequences which follow. You need to know that the process of transitional change and adjustment to the new may last much longer than you would expect or have prepared for.

You do not want to become like those who have lost sight and feel that they have failed at their personal goal or professional mission in the new country. You want to know that in order to adapt successfully to the new circumstances, you already have thought through your true motivation for the change you have been planning. Once you have defined your motivation, the process of transition will become bearable and meaningful and, above all, challenging, in a positive way.

During this 'new' life, you will find that almost everything refers to your initial motivation for emigration, as this motivation is the basis on which you will have built your developing outcome – your present and your future. Building a new life constructively or breaking down – sometimes even intentionally – will depend on the fundamental starting point.

Was that starting point solid, clearly defined and commonly agreed? Or, was it unclear, undefined and shaky? The problem usually lies in the unfortunate fact that the initial shakiness will only be diagnosed once the transitional period becomes too much for the individual to handle. The reason for this often stems from the fact that the decision, and everything contributing to the decision-making process, was not clearly defined.

Most experts on transitional change agree that the starting point is definition. The significance of this should never be underestimated. William Bridges, an expert in the field says that 'definition' is not only phrasing something in words, but it is something that actually impacts on orientation and the process of restructuring.[1]

Orientation refers to a structured life with a career plan and clear goal setting, as well as the periphery of emotional, social and spiritual experiences that accompany such orientation. Restructuring refers to an ongoing process of evaluation regarding those variables, or things, that you are continuously confronted with, and which need to be tackled in the most effective way, all the time.

This is a necessary skill to have right through the course of transition, and is vital for allowing yourself to grow and develop into the successful being you initially had in mind for yourself. No matter what your specific defined outcome in the new country is, whether it be as a successful career person, or perhaps to create a better family life and safer home circumstances, change touches us all in one way or another, whoever or wherever we are. Systems theory, with its known feature: 'the whole is more than the sum of its parts', offers some explanation in this regard.

One aspect of personal change that features significantly during the process of emigration and settling into a new country, is that the individual, who experiences major change, indirectly influences those around him – their surroundings as well as their personal functioning. The effect, however, is straightforward and direct.

The impact of change, in many respects, resembles the ripple effect when you throw a pebble into a pond of water – the circles run wider and wider, slowly and continuously, as if everlasting. Look at the sea. Hear its roar. See the waves rolling on an on, creating change as time goes on. Feel its effect on life outside the waters, demanding individuals and communities to make changes.

In life, if the individual makes a major life change, it ripples through and affects others within his immediate setting, whether it is at work, family or within his social circle. It asks for change, whether in attitude or in behaviour. It is a reciprocal process, and one that depends largely on the way it will be dealt with by all those who are involved in this process. It directs not only yours, but also others' opinions, feelings, choices and behaviour.

The direction and drive in our life is usually determined by our perception of the world around us, and by the internal maps of this external world that we are creating for ourselves. These maps are crucial when it comes to dealing with the issues of relocation.

The initial decision of where we eventually will be heading with our lives is therefore a very subjective stand to depart from, embedded in a perception. This perception could be predetermined by the effect that our past experiences have had had on us, and how these have interacted with the dreams that we cuddle in our minds, eventually leading to our actions and reactions.

Whether these reactions are physical or emotional, they establish the specific orientation mentioned earlier. They would set the point of departure of the journey of our continuous development in a new country, or perhaps on our eventual return to our country of origin.

In this context, orientation and perception are almost synonymous. Some writers differentiate between the cognitive element and the emotional role that certain stimuli from your environment have on your perceptions. This will in turn lead to a certain choice of behaviour.

The consequences of the behaviour that you have chosen will explain how you come to understand and represent the world around you, while your emotional (or affective) disposition focuses on how you relate to that world. Therefore, there is focus on both the emotions and thinking. These two concepts become vital ingredients during the process of change, especially when you look for ways to deal with the new situation, new events, a new life within the context of this book, it refers specifically to how you cope with new challenges, events and traumas.

I trust that this book, which covers most of these aspects, will help you to deal with this event in your life, not only from the time that you make the decision to emigrate, until you feel settled in, but also afterwards, as change is ongoing and ever-present, almost omni-present.

The reason for looking at the psychology involved in making a change, is because psychology is part and parcel of everyday human life and therefore not only for the academic studying in psychology. It is also for the man on the street – every woman, man and child everywhere, and at any given time.

The book not only refers to the personal experiences of different people, but also draws on the psychology of personal and transitional change of individuals and families, who are undergoing the process of adjustment and resettling into a new country. We shall see how some of the theories underlying these processes reveal themselves in reality.

When it comes to families, we learn how such important units stick together – or fall apart. We know that families usually have their own ways of dealing with situations and stressful circumstances in general, but a major change like emigration often rocks a family, sometimes for the better, and quite often, for the worse.

You will discover the impact of the different phases of transitional change caused by emigration or relocation, on the many different developmental stages and phases of individuals within a family, and also the stage in the family's life cycle during these processes.

Indeed, it is a time to be acutely aware of your family members as individuals and to realize that your own individuality still exists, but that you are also part of the family, as a unit or a system. This will play a major role in the transitional process and eventually, in the success of settling down.

Therefore, we are looking at different people, individuals and families and learning from their experiences, in order to know more and be better prepared for what lies ahead.

We will also cover stress. Stress is part and parcel of life and can interfere significantly with the process of transition and settling down. The way a person deals with stress may also dictate how they will adjust and move through the transitional process. Stress is therefore dealt with extensively, so that you can understand why certain things happen to you and your loved ones, despite your hard attempts to make things work.

You might feel at some stage that there has been some kind of failure somewhere along the way. Or, you wonder why some people seem to thrive on stress and pressure and are more adaptable to change than others. When discussing the effect of stress on the brain, it is not a certainty that if you suffer from stress you are, or might become, psychologically unbalanced.

Rather, it refers to how certain functions of the brain are influenced and affected by stress, and what exactly causes the distress and biopsychological reactions when you are exposed to a new life in a foreign country.

To know the underlying reasons is to understand everything so much better. Understanding brings along acceptance that there are acknowledgeable reasons for certain decisions and patterns of behaviour. This can make a change in behaviour so much easier to accept, especially when you know you have to change some of your ways. Very often, also your beliefs and values need to be changed in order to adjust successfully to your new circumstances.

Contributing to your happiness in a new location and world that you are creating for yourself, is the significant role that emotional, spiritual and social intelligence will be playing. To help develop this fascinating part of you we shall deal with this in practical ways, also through written exercises, or activities.

If you prefer not to do these activities, you may miss out on the full experience of getting to know yourself better. And to know yourself, would be a basic starting point from where you depart when you want to leave your heimat to settle into your new country successfully.

You may find that your ultimate destination may not lie in the city in which you have arrived, but most likely in a place and at a time that you will define at some point in the future. Somewhere very personal, and deep within you.

Chapter 2
Considering the issues involved

Is it not true that thoughts have a funny way of sticking, clinging and spreading through your mind once you allow their existence? Not only do they tend to take the shape of something different and promising, but, very often, they merge into an 'unreal' reality - a reality which subconsciously guides you towards making certain decisions and eventually, guiding you towards specific actions as a consequence of that decision.

The move to another country may be something like that - that conception of the thought might have already taken place some time ago, often unconsciously. Perhaps you have allowed it to grow and develop into something upfront in your mind. Nevertheless, eventually you have to face it: you are trying to give up the known for the unknown, despite the consequences involved.

Pondering the idea will do no harm, but reacting to vague thoughts about moving far away, or abroad, followed by impulsive actions such as giving up your job, saying your goodbyes as quickly as possible and buying that one-way ticket, can become regrettable, especially if you have family responsibilities.

Of course, there is also the flipside of the coin, but you need to realize that the pitfalls are real and will have to be dealt with on an ongoing basis. You can do only this if you really understand what they are about. You also need to understand and acknowledge your own motivation and abilities, in order to avoid regrettable decisions based on vague ideas and distant dreams.

Where did it start?

Relocating is a process, which contains all the different elements and phases of the process of transitional change. This process will impact significantly on you and on your loved ones over a period of time, and it will affect both those people you take with you, and those who stay behind.

So... where did your idea to emigrate really start?

It is not surprising, and nothing new, that often the process of relocating begins with daydreaming about the new country and the excitement that surrounds the idea of relocation. Perhaps you were inspired by other people's stories about their experiences abroad, or maybe your wandering mind is seeking excitement and fulfillment somewhere else. (Does the familiar phrase 'the grass is always greener on the other side' ring a bell?)

So, where should you start once you know that you are interested in such change? Firstly, you look at the real reasons for wanting to move. Those inner, unspoken reasons that most of the time form part of a hidden, suppressed self-talk in the subconscious mind. Or, should we say in the unconscious mind?

Underlying the success of trustworthy evaluation of the pros and cons you are facing, is self-honesty based on scrupulous introspection. Often this is easier said than done, as there is seldom anything as strong as those defense mechanisms which we tend to mobilise when we feel threatened by our own emotions; those times when we tend to see only what we want to see.

These emotions are usually so powerful that they may become too frightening and often too painful to deal with. In such situations, people tend to suppress their emotions to their subconscious and unconscious mind and start to construct 'more acceptable' ways of handling the difficult task ahead.

With regard to moving abroad, a person may, for instance, create for himself an acceptable world in an attempt to minimize or underplay the demands and uncertainties of the new, especially in explaining why he is leaving his own country and loved ones. Often he will rationalize and justify his decisions to make them more acceptable to himself and to others.

You would know that it is easy to get lost in the joy and excitement of learning all about your chosen country – especially when you visualize yourself in these new surroundings, telling your friends and family about the fascinating, different world they can only dream about.

Or perhaps it is about you, the explorer and investigator who had the courage to pluck up roots - something about you that others probably can only admire and wish they could share. Guts, perhaps?

Or, maybe you want to start afresh and have a new life in another place, far away from memories and the red tape and boredom of ordinary, day-to-day life. Or, there is a career opportunity you dare not let pass.

Some people say they emigrate to expose their children to a different culture and to broaden their horizons. For many it is a real situation of finding better education and career opportunities than their country of origin can offer.

Having lived in London for some time now, I have had the opportunity to interview many people who have fled their countries and found asylum in Britain; people who have been traumatized by a background of political unrest, war and general instability. For many, finding that new peace has simultaneously brought about new confrontation, characterized by the turmoil of ongoing inner processes, which are war zones in their own right.

The tidal wave of East Europeans to Britain, Mid-Africans to South Africa, and many more, even Britons, to and from other continents is proof in many respects of the desperate search for financial security and a life worth living.

A common factor amongst many individuals, despite their different backgrounds, culture and beliefs, especially in Britain, are of course, money. As round, golden and heavy as the valued little pound may seem, just as strong is its attraction, especially if one pound counts for many of your own country's monetary units.

However, as a point of departure in this life-changing journey, you must be clear about the real reason why you want to leave your heimat. For this, you must be able to look deeply into yourself and be able to word and verbalize your thoughts - even if you do not like them.

Risk and reason

Basic to all understanding of being human is the fact that you are part of a bigger world, a world that you tend to fragmentize into several different categories of 'worlds' or areas of existence. However, these cannot be separated from one another, as they are all connected and overlapping.

These can also be referred to as the different parts of your life in which you have certain roles to fulfill. Such a thought may be soothing, but also frightening, as it holds major and far-reaching consequences. It is when you look back on these consequences that you see how they have resulted from the initial choices that you made.

To be part of the whole of your own life means that you have to take risks, and accept the consequences following those risks you dare to take – almost on a daily basis. With that in mind, you also, at certain times, may choose to withdraw from such responsibility, or attempt to put it on hold. Probably because you think you can afford to postpone decision-making – procrastination such as 'I'll see...' or 'let someone else decide' or 'my partner will take the lead in selling our house.'

Perhaps you do not agree that you have distanced yourself from such responsibilities, just as you have distanced yourself from those you love. But then I must ask you, why do you deny that you are part of your immediate world? Perhaps it is because it may sometimes be too confrontational or challenging to acknowledge that there are things which are too difficult to handle at a certain time? Like telling your family that you are moving abroad, never to return?

Or, is it that things have become too stressful for your own psychological capacity to absorb and work through? Perhaps you have misinterpreted your level of emotional hardiness? If so, it is not the end of the world. You will discover by reading this book that many people tend to miss or misinterpret the clues their own minds offer to assist them in making the right decision at the right time.

Those who address these issues are those who will win the battle. And it is during this process that you learn to develop your psychological hardiness and emotional intelligence, in order to adjust to your new circumstances and to achieve your long-term goals.

I have listened to people who did not have the courage to tell their friends or family that they want to leave for good. The reason for this is understandable, but in some ways unthinkable. They do not want to consider the impact of their departure on those who are staying behind, because facing their possible distraught reactions could jeopardize their plans to leave – or stir up unbearable guilt and blame. Thereby not thinking of the others, but rather of themselves.

They prefer to choose the easier way by just focusing on the physical issues of emigration, and leave dealing with the emotional side untouched. This has led to a situation in which they start to focus on the so-called negative things about their present situation, and they move into a state of mind where rationalizing their decision become almost a lifestyle. They easily find their willing victims of blame: politics, crime and economy.

Because some of these people easily fall into the rhythm of other people's ideas and beliefs, due to their preferred and purposeful susceptibility, they try to convince themselves and their family how bad their home country really is, and that a better future can only be found elsewhere. They revel in bad news on the television about the country they have left behind, as this, in their mind, confirms that they have made the right decision to have left. I often hear how people, who have been in England for some years, still bad-mouth their home country and its problems.

Therefore, they actually try to soothe themselves into thinking that they have made the right decision not to return. It is as if they are looking for reasons to make their initial decision appear acceptable, or, even worse, to use it as a way to deal with their actual longing and yearning to return home.

What an ineffective way to attempt to solve a problem, you might say. Still, how many people do not fool themselves in this way, and therefore degrade their own lives to prevent a self-actualization and self-fulfillment which might have otherwise developed.

Sometimes people do not consider the emotional side of the issue, because they still doubt their plan to leave. Have they really made the right choice? What if things do not work out?

It is in many respects a completely different situation for asylum seekers and refugees who indeed have to consider and acknowledge the traumatic impact of their countries' political unrest and socio-economic instability. They mostly have to make hard and unwelcome decisions as their families' safety is at stake.

For them, the decision to leave is sometimes the only realistic option. However, it is still hard to apply, as it entails permanent and forced goodbyes, because along with other traumas, moving into an unknown future means leaving with nothing and arriving with even less.

The trauma faced by asylum seekers unfortunately falls beyond the scope of this book, as the issues they have to deal with are, in fact, a study of their own. However, as you read on and see what impact stress can have in uncertain circumstances, you will realize how great the impact would be on asylum seekers – people from countries where there are never-ending, life-threatening conditions of fear and hunger, strangling the last bit of spirit, and leaving them with no other option than to flee a country they once cherished. We can name several such countries: Iraq, Iran, Afghanistan, Kosovo, Zimbabwe.

On the brighter side, there are students and young people who often influence one another with their dreams of a 'more exiting and promising world,' which they feel they need to experience in order to expand and develop their world and personality.

Those who can afford to leave a country temporarily are lucky, but is this really the only way in which a person can develop? Do you need to leave at a young age? Should you not wait until you have obtained your degree or diploma? Or, do you by any chance rationalize it, like so many; by saying you have to go now to benefit your C.V. for the future?

What exactly do you want to write on your C.V.? How you have traveled and worked abroad, in different places on short-term contracts, some not even lasting a month?

Or, is it rather for the expansion of your mindset, which will eventually enrich you as a person to such an extent that you will understand things better, and eventually develop the skill of appreciation?

Indeed, travel can be such a broadening experience. What is interesting is that quite often, it is only at some strange point in your life, at the most unexpected moment, that you suddenly recognize it as such.

And when it happens, the feeling of enlightenment can be overwhelming and intensely liberating. There is a feeling of completion, contentment, and of coming home to the self within. You are embracing your whole being with the love and compassion you have been searching for so long.

Readiness

One of the vital ingredients for successful adjustment to a new country is recognizing when you are ready to make the change. If you still seek reassurance from others about your decision, then you are not yet ready to make the move. If this is the case, then you should rethink everything again.

The fact that you will have to 'stand on your own two feet' once you are in a new country is not only an expression; it is a very real experience. It is as alone as being in a witness box, testifying and undergoing painful cross-examination.

To arrive in another country all alone, is in many ways to meet the unknown you at the airport, instead of some stranger who has come to collect you. In many circumstances this will be something that you will only realize in retrospect, at a much later stage.

But, of course, nothing goes without excitement and wide-eyed wonder, and it definitely deserves a pat on the shoulder too. You have made it to Heathrow, JFK International Airport, Hong Kong or Vancouver – or wherever your dreams or work have taken you. You have already survived the first challenge, which is to say goodbye in order to arrive. You may be surprised to learn that your destination may not be the city you have just arrived in, but most likely at a place and time that you will eventually define for yourself at some time in the future. Somewhere very personal and deep within you.

How you will have arrived will depend largely on how you have approached life's challenges and demands; specifically, how you have chosen to react in certain situations and circumstances. You know that you cannot always change certain situations or a specific event, but you can choose how you are going to deal with and react to it. Having made that choice, you will have to take responsibility for its consequences. In this way, you control your destiny.

Challenges

During the process of adaptation to the new, based upon the ongoing nature of transitional change, you will find that your new country will offer numerous situations of continuous transitional factors that you will have to address. Not only in the new job that you are trying to manage, but also in your personal life and that of your loved ones, as they also need to learn how to cope with the changes initiated and driven by you.

After almost a decade in England, I still feel that the greatest challenge I have ever faced is moving here permanently, at least at this stage. And the challenges are still rolling in, one after the other, asking, no, *begging*, me to deal with them. It is as if life has become a challenge in itself. (Mostly positive, I must say.)

By 'begging', I mean that I have to acknowledge that there are still times and situations when I feel confronted with the memory of the emotional comfort of the past. I have to recognize and acknowledge that it is those memories which could lead to impulsive decisions such as packing up and returning home. But luckily (and this is a big but), the human mind is a thinking mind, and you have set long-term goals to work towards. Acknowledging this usually prevents impulsive actions.

But how do you define the word 'challenge'? It is, of course, a concept based on a person's perceptions and, therefore, quite personal. But eventually, it is about you and your understanding of the processes you have become involved with, when you initially made that choice to relocate to a place far away.

Here is a written exercise to help throw some light on the practicalities awaiting you at different stages of relocation. This will help you to clarify your thoughts, as a prerequisite to your personal change management style, which is crucial to the process of resettlement.

Exercise 1: (add more pages if necessary)

(i) Write down your definition of the word 'challenge'.

....
....
....
....
....
....

(ii) Now analyse it further by looking it up in different dictionaries.

....
....
....
....
....
....
....
....
....
....
....
....
....
....

(iii) Write down some of these definitions and compare them to your initial definition

....
....
....
....
....
....
....

(iv) Do you want to change your definition of the word?

....
....
....
....
....
....
....
....
....

(v)　If so, why? If not, why not?

....
....
....
....
....
....
....
....
....
....
....

(vi) Write down your new definition of the word

....
....
....
....
....
....
....
....
....
....

(vii) Describe how you feel about your new definition

....
....
....
....
....
....
....
....
....
....

The Encarta® World English Dictionary's definition of the word 'challenge' is as follows:

Invite: to invite somebody to participate in a fight, contest, or competition.

Dare: to dare somebody to do something, to call something into question by demanding an explanation, justification, or proof.

Stimulate: to stimulate somebody by making demands on the intellect.

Order: to order somebody to stop and produce identification or a password, law object to inclusion of juror, to make a formal objection against the inclusion of a prospective juror on a jury; immunology test whether something produces allergy: to expose a person or animal to a substance in order to determine whether an allergy or other adverse reaction will occur[2].

When you think about these different meanings, you may hear a tone ringing, or even trace a certain pattern. It is almost like being dared into a certain something, something that may entail conflicting thoughts and feelings. It may refer to demands for certain reactions, as it clearly asks you to stretch your abilities beyond the usual cognitive and emotional capabilities. It is beyond the known emotional equipment of the past, equipment that would have been applied readily and successfully in certain circumstances.

But on this new occasion, like your emigration, you may find that the known equipment may suddenly have become outdated or insufficient. Therefore, a 'challenge' seems to be something with special features, something dynamic and mostly changeable without being flexible.

It will be you, however, who will have to be flexible and creative in your choice of suitable reactions to those demands made upon you. Should you become aware that your usual equipment fails the situation, you would also become aware of the dynamics that follow.

The inflexibility I mentioned refers to the fact that although it may look different at different times, its main feature stays the same, namely resettling in a new country.

The Encarta® definition states that 'challenge' also means to stimulate somebody by making demands upon the intellect. This becomes clear when you move through the process of relocation, which is a process of transitional change, on a very personal basis. It is one where both the emotions and the intellect play very important roles, especially the different levels of intelligence, as the 'big change' is often something far beyond our expectations.

Often you leave with a dream and arrive with expectation, but instead, you meet confusion. You may even find painful frustration. You experience the depth of loss. It is then when you will delve into your inner self and will discover your strengths – and you will know that you have to move on, despite those unwelcome surprises and daunting disillusionments.

Chapter 3
Transitional change beyond expectation

Thinking about the prospective changes that I would have been forced to make once we started the emigration process, was a given. I had accepted that there would be lots of changes for me to deal with, for my family members individually, for us as a family unit, and no doubt, for our families of origin, too.

I could not help that the inner message from somewhere in my professional background of psychology and social work, would transpire actively throughout my process of emigration. It reminded me of the traffic light process, which is ongoing by way of its flickering red and yellow lights until, eventually, the green light appears.

Within the process of emigration, the change of colours can take immensely long, and the flickering can make you dizzy and feeling sick, and sometimes patience almost run out before the green light makes its appearance. You also know that you should not start going before the green is not steadily there, right in front of you, telling it is now safe to move forward. But then you often do just that – start to walk or drive before the time is right, with disastrous consequences.

You also know that whichever way you obey the changing colours of your traffic light, there are processes involved in every one of them.

This knowledge has featured all the way during our emigration – knowledge that, whichever way we look at how change will and can affect us, there will be both psychological and social processes of considerable effect, and that we will most certainly have to face stressful situations, those moments and periods of the yellow and red lights of our new life. I also knew that we would have the strength to endure them, because we wanted to.

However, I think that it was only when I was in the situation that its full impact struck me, and only at that point did I realize how deeply it had cut, both emotionally and cognitively.

I know that a person is always developing and changing, and that we never become too old to learn. And, I know that we move through different phases of the process of development. All of these phases are processes in their own right: from pre-birth through to adolescence, and through adulthood into old age.

But the fact that the transitions accompanying change accentuate the concept of on-the-move to such an extent, that the bridging periods can become fields of war and play in their own right, almost bowled me over.

Luckily, I discovered what theory has shown all the time. It is by approaching this major life event realistically, and with a clear mind, that one's organizational abilities and systematic ways of problem-solving make their appearance in different ways –important tools for putting up tent in another country.

To understand the emotional process involved in transitional change will ease this process significantly, but it would not necessarily simplify it. Therefore looking at change and transition on a deeper level is essential.

Change and transition

You have to realize and admit that change is as continuous as breathing. It is a natural thing. Like someone once said: 'the only stable thing about change is that change is not a stable thing'. Change occurs around you just as it is happening within you, all the time. Just as the stars in the sky are dying and new ones are being born, as the daffodil dies just to sprout out again next year, filling fields and gardens with its narcissistic beauty and promise of summer: such is the impact of change on you and your life.

Similarly, the cells in your body are dying off, shedding outdated and used parts whilst, in the meantime, the body actively and miraculously creates new enzymes and cells all the time. This creation of change happens throughout your life, and also on other levels. In your social and psychological life, change also occurs continuously, some minor and other major, but one is not necessarily less significant than the other.

However, the change brought about by relocation and emigration, with its challenging consequences of having to settle in unknown circumstances, will require specific psychological and mental attitudes that could be detrimental if you choose ineffective coping styles.

Your mental attitude and related psychological processes will influence your thoughts, which, in turn, will dictate your actions and reactions. In reality, it becomes a process of specialized, purposeful management of your own life.

How you do this successfully, depends on your willingness to scrupulously look at the changes brought about by emigration, from different perspectives. You have to do so to get an idea of how you might react to the changes that you are going to make.

If you are already in your new location, you might like to know and understand why you have reacted to your emigration in certain ways since the first day of arrival. You need to consider the significance of transitional change from not only an intellectual, cognitive point of view, but also, and especially, from an emotional viewpoint.

Not emotional in the sense that you allow your emotions to tint and distort your rational thinking, but in the sense of emotionality, in terms of the psychological impact that the process of change entails.

As change contains transitions with very specific features linked to it, you have to address these features on an ongoing basis, as they will be popping out in many different forms, at different times, and in different circumstances. These features are discussed in the following chapters.

Change and transition are not the same

Although change and transition may appear to be the same, experts in the field of change management differentiate between the two concepts.

William Bridges[3] states that change happens suddenly, in one moment, and that transition, on the other hand, takes time. He voices what I, and many others, have experienced since we decided to move abroad: that transition is an ongoing, internal process that you go through in order to come to terms with the change that already had happened at some time in the past.

'If you move from California to New York City, the change is crossing the country and learning your way around the Big Apple…Transition is different. The starting point for transition is not the outcome but the ending that you will have to make to leave the old situations behind.' (William Bridges, p.4)

He explains that situational change hinges on the new thing, and that psychological transition depends on letting go of the old reality and the old identity you had before the change took place. How this idea works in practice, can be seen in the following chapters where we will look at individual experiences of the process of relocation.

Transition therefore indicates moving from one domain to another, on an emotional level when emotional changes will occur, guiding you towards another aspect of your personality. Often, this will be in addition to the existing one, and its ways of dealing with life's demands.

However, these changes do not always happen on a linear basis, with clear-cut boundaries between phases, and a distinctive start and end point. They overlap, and can be diffused.

Unfortunately, this is not always what people expect. They think they can and will, just like that, draw a line behind the past and start afresh before the time for doing so is right for them. They are eager to adjust and settle in.

Then, all too often, the difficulties that come alongside the process of the big change will bring along emotional upheaval and disappointment. These difficulties may postpone or even prevent happiness in the new situation. People tend to leave their country of origin feeling excited about a new life abroad, float on the initial cloud of euphoria that new surroundings can bring, and then be in shock at the raw reality when it sinks in.

Many people discover that the job agent who recruited them has twisted the truth about their new job or lied to them shamelessly, or that their understanding of what being 'professional' is, differs completely to that of their new employer and colleagues.

Many experience endless frustrations both in the workplace and socially, especially when they realize that others expect them to adapt quickly, and let go of their own ideas, beliefs and values almost straight away. Most of the time these are values which have contributed to their identity and the decision to emigrate. They find it extremely hard to let go, and experience intense emotional and professional loss.

But eventually, many will discover their inner strength, and will consciously decide to move with the flow of change. They are still the same people, but in many ways not the same.

Life cycles

The psychological impact of change stretches even further. It also relates to life cycles, because a person's bio-socio-psychological development takes him through different stages and cycles, each with its own delights, issues and challenges.

In addition to this, when you add significant demographic changes like moving to another country, you realize that all of these things are extensively intertwined, and that specific intervention and purposeful self-assessment may be required in order to deal with the process of transitional change effectively. It will form part of your life story, and if you are able to look at yourself in time, so that you can learn from it, you will gain significantly.

By analyzing the meaning of certain events in your life up to this point, your reactions, connections and chosen behaviour, and the link between all of these, it will reveal certain patterns in your life that are running across time.

These patterns may be certain types of behaviour, similar choices made within certain circumstances or other events happening in your life. Sometimes there is sense in these patterns, other times they plead for change, if only you were willing to look at the recognizable elements and realize the need to break some of these patterns.

You have to decide if you want to continue maintaining the same patterns that you are discovering in the process, or whether you want to change them by making different choices now, and in the future.

You should keep in mind that your interpretation of the meaning of transitional change, and its link with the stages of change within individual life cycles, will affect you and your dear ones, in many different ways. No matter what their circumstances, age or nature, no two people will deal with transitional change in the same way, or experience the same losses, pain and challenges that come with change, similarly.

No two people share the same tempo of growth and development. Maintaining this realization requires ongoing respect for what it means to be human.

Chapter 4
Cyclic challenges of the big change

To have good emotional health you have to maintain compassion, not only for your loved ones, but also for yourself. You need to look at yourself with acceptance, love and understanding, not only when you face the traumas, excitement and challenges of emigration change, but also in your life in general. During the process of emigration this becomes even more necessary.

It is by doing so, that you will continue to realize that your big change requires willingness and commitment to know and understand the nature and demands that transitional change holds.

Cycles of change

Zooming in on any new circumstance or situation, you will see many features of the process of change that are similar to other personal changing circumstances, if not almost identical.

Psychologists and others in related professions have, over time, developed a number of different models to explain the process of change. Central and common to these models is the fact that when people want to, or have to, change, there will always be specific elements linked to the process and its specific stages, that you will go through, and have to deal with before you can move on.

To do this successfully, you need to address the way you think, because your thinking largely dictates your behaviour, and this, you will find, is a cycle in its own right.

Making a change means addressing your feelings, thoughts, relationships and behaviour (to mention just a few). It also means to alter and adjust these. If you are not willing to alter your thinking after certain major life events and change of circumstances, your emotional life may be disastrous or destructive, as there will be lots of loose ends that you will have to deal with.

Man is meant to grow and develop, to move forward, and to progress to fulfillment. To become stuck in the process of transitional change without the willpower and energy to overcome the obstacles and challenges on this road, would be to avoid your responsibility to yourself and those around you, especially those who are emotionally close to you.

Research has already confirmed that this is indeed a challenging road to travel, and so have many people also experienced. They have found that the cycle of change can easily absorb you, and you may find that too – that it wants to trip you, handicap you, and absorb you. But it is self-understanding and motivation that will help you move through the stages more smoothly, that is to say, if you deal with the tasks set at every stage; and what is more, that you complete these psychological tasks. They address emotional processes.

Professionals who have worked with people who are addicted to substances confirm this. They will tell you that although drug addiction can claim your life mentally, emotionally and physically, and recovery is always very, very hard, such recovery is indeed possible.[4]

During rehabilitation, addicts learn that there are different stages in the process of recovery, and that you can get stuck during any of these stages. They also learn that during this process you may relapse, start again, relapse again, and with enough motivation, you will eventually succeed and maintain a new, substance-free lifestyle.

But there is a condition. Motivation must be an inner, self-motivational drive, because it is you who wants to change. You do it yourself, by yourself, and for yourself – not for someone else.

This also applies to your big change. It works in exactly the same way during your adjustment to life in a new country, and it will be the case even if your emigration was self-chosen, selective and positively motivated.

Why? Because you will find yourself in the cyclic process of moving back and forth, from phase to phase – of lapsing and relapsing until you eventually will have reached emotional closure. The process will require that you deal with each phase specifically and complete its demands. This is necessary to ensure that you are really ready to move on to the next stage.

It is much more than just changing the physical circumstances of where you live. Rather, it refers to the emotional processes involved. Remember, as we said, that your new address is not just a telephone call away, it is actually miles of emotional cycles away. Emotional miles, which can shrink and stretch depending on how well you deal with the issues involved.

The reciprocal nature of cycles and phases

A cycle is like a spiral. When it comes to the process of personal transitional change, this spiral may stretch and shrink, appearing differently every time you look at it from another angle.

Just look the next time when you hold a spiraled wire in your hand. Look at it and feel it. It moves, but it also rigid. The original point stays in shape in the same place. When you hold one end of the wire in your hand and pull at the other end, you can push it in, bend it or keep it clamped; it moves and changes face. Let go at one end and it reverts back to its original form and position. Does this not remind you of elasticity, without being elastic?

Imagine moving up or down this spiral. You can see the spaces or loops, which you go through, and you realize that you cannot ignore them like when you are running up the stairs, two or three steps at a time. You know that once you are in the loop, you cannot escape without being affected in one way or another.

Psychological stages and phases are very similar. Although you cannot separate one stage totally from the other, as they are overlapping and intertwined, you can differentiate between them by recognizing certain thoughts, behaviour and emotions, which are quite specific or typical to a certain stage.

During one's life span, there are stages when you experience several forms of the process happening within you – often at the same time. These have been closely linked to your personal circumstances and experiences during certain times and events in your life. To emigrate and resettle in a new country, or a completely different place from what you have been used to, is an event, which highlights these processes, and which tests your psychological ability to actively deal with them. In the end, you could find that it has both accommodated and nurtured your emotional and spiritual growth.

There is no set tempo against which you will move between the stages and phases. It is an individual thing, and very personal. It will depend on your individual circumstances, personality, psychological hardiness, and motivation.

Some immigrants in England told me that it had taken them about four to five years before they felt that they had completed the process. For others, it had taken much longer. Some seem to have never reached closure. For most single people without too much emotional baggage, the process appears to be much easier. Again, people's differences in reacting and processing information internally should not be ignored. What works for one person now may only work for another person at a later date.

There are several developmental theories explaining your psychosocial development during the separate, but overlapping, individual phases, that face you over your lifespan. One commonly known theory in developmental psychology is that of the psychotherapist, Erik Erikson, who emphasized the socio-cultural determinants of personality in his theory of psychosocial development.[5]

He accentuates the importance of completing one stage before you can successfully move on to the next. If your needs in a certain stage have not been met, they may resurface some time later in life, often unexpectedly.

Children whose needs for unconditional acceptance and love have not been met sufficiently, may, for example, struggle to deal with meaningful relationships during their adult years. They will still have to address those issues stemming from initial rejection, at some time in the future. It will mean carrying the emotional aftermath of childhood through their adult lives with the ongoing feeling of not belonging, of standing on the sideline.

These unresolved issues often continue through several future relationships, and will continue to urge the owner to address the underlying issues, and to actively try to resolve them. Indeed, this is something that is possible, if you really want to change your life for the better.

If you thought that these individual phases and stages are enough to deal with, there are more. There are life cycles of relationships and family life, as significant in their meaning and impact on its members as there are individual issues involved. This implies that you should attentively consider your children's ages and the associated stages of their development, as well as that of your partner or spouse, when you consider a major change in you and your family's lives, especially if you plan to move abroad.

Additional processes

There are more to consider. In addition to the individual and family developmental phases, there is also the process of loss. Loss has its own characteristics involving stages, phases and emotional tasks linked to each specific stage. These are intertwined with the flow of the previously discussed developmental stages of your life.

The impact of loss will be discussed extensively in a separate chapter, because the experience of loss plays a major role in transitional change. This is especially hard and heartfelt during the course of migration and relocation.

What then is the process of change? It consists of several stages: from pre-contemplation through to contemplation, preparation, action and maintenance, and includes relapse, which can happen at any time until the full cycle has been completed and the changed entity (for example a new behaviour pattern like stopping smoking, because you are thinking differently about it) has been established.

It is amazing to see when looking at a deeper level, that the features of the process of change are also present in other developmental phases. In every one of these phases there may also be characteristics of a previous stage, like in the overall process of planning to emigrate, actively moving abroad, settling in, and maintaining the new life. Once you are in a new country you may find yourself in another cycle, while the phase of settling in may involve the same processes as the overall process. Therefore, you could say that you have cycles within cycles.

On your journey to understand what you are going through during the transitional change of relocation, you may like to start by addressing this process first. In discussing each phase separately, we shall address two scenarios: firstly, the overall process, and secondly, the situation when you are already in the new location.

Pre-contemplation

Recall the first time when the thought of relocating to another country crossed your mind. At that stage, it was not a necessity or important enough for you to act on it immediately. You pushed the thought aside, suppressed the idea and left it for later. You were comfortable in your lifestyle and surroundings, and did not see a reason to really make that change.

Others would talk about relocation or emigration, and although you were not cold to the thought, you could leave it alone. You might have become aware of the idea as a possible and available option, and gradually, perhaps you would have become more acquainted with the idea.

This may be pre-contemplation, the first phase in the cycle of change.

There are no clear-cut images in your mind yet, and no new moves planned or made.

In the different scenario of you having lived in the new country for some time, you will be able to look back and realize how even the next phase of contemplation, which you have already entered by then, or have moved through, held within it its own fragments of pre-contemplation. It is as if you are being pulled and held back by some psychological force within you. You just do not always recognize it at the time.

Perhaps you still needed that feeling at that stage, as if it is helping you to maintain your identity – the identity that you know and are familiar with. But as the process moves on, your feelings change, sometimes continuously, as they are influenced by numerous factors, mostly on a deeper, emotional level.

These feelings could have psychological reasons, or they could stem from your social world – how well your family has adjusted to the changes that you have initiated, or something physical in the new circumstances. You will look back and experience how intertwined and linked the different stages of transitional change are to those of loss.

By now, you have realized that you have to adjust to everything new, or perhaps it is the same job, but the cultural surroundings so different - sometimes shockingly so. No matter how hard you try, periodically you may find that you still long for the past, think of going back and plan secret strategies as to when and how you are going to do it. You keep that back door slightly open, just in case. However, you may have also realized by now that it is better to stay: for all the right reasons!

Acknowledging this conflict as a reality of the state of your psyche at a specific stage is to acknowledge that you are not yet ready to let go of the past, or at least, not ready at that specific point in your life. You have to allow this new realization, and you should deal with the feelings involved in it. Otherwise, you may get stuck emotionally.

You have to mark the ending of a previous phase before embarking upon the next.

It could be difficult because, in your mind, your emotional security still lies in the past. In that case, you will still be living there, too. The words of a Turkish woman one cold, rainy afternoon in London's Canning Town echoed exactly that. She said that she did not want to change any of her interior decoration in the new home, as the old furniture (especially soft furnishings brought from Turkey) were a reminder of a past time filled with happiness and security.

'The colours have faded because they are so old, yet, in my heart they will always stay bright and beautiful...

'We've been here a couple of years now, yet, in my mind I'm still back home, every day of my life. It is tearing me apart. I just cannot move on. I'm still sleeping under my old duvet. Yes, I know I can find a better one here, but I do not want it. I want mine.'

In the beginning, when you try to settle in, maintaining some of your old home's decor can also be a positive way of ensuring a feeling of continuity, especially for your children. They may need the emotional security of some known material things around them like bedding, the familiar smell of detergents in their clothes, and the aroma of known food – anything, that reminds them of home.

I remember a friend telling me about her three year-old daughter, whose ecstatic joy was completely overwhelming when, after two months of waiting for their furniture and belongings to arrive in London, they started unpacking and her daughter suddenly noticed her favourite old rag doll peeping out from underneath the other items. It is not necessary to say how deep emotions were running in that house that night – especially for mum and dad, who have entered a time in their lives where their old rag doll could stay hidden in the misty clouds of emigration loss.

But time moves on. No one has to tell you that. You try hard to keep your emotions in check, but still, as the sun sets over the Thames and

Canary Wharf and the mist starts rolling in, you look up into the sky and ask for strength. And you find it.

You try to work on friendships. Yet, still, you may find that you are reluctant to make friends on a deeper emotional level, because you still cuddle your old ones in your mind, as if you are going to see them again next week. You may struggle with feelings of disloyalty and are scared that you may lose your old friends if you let go of the past. It is almost like an internal war, as if you cannot enjoy the new and old together, as if new friends are threatening your love and loyalty towards the old ones.

You may feel that if you really settle in the new country you will be faced with the danger of growing apart from your old friends. You may experience intense fear that you are going to lose out, and that your loved ones may die before you can return home.

These feelings often drift just below consciousness, and do not always surface as specific emotions observable by others. Sometimes you have not even defined them – you are just aware of a feeling of ongoing sadness, even bewilderment, at times.

It often happens when elderly parents stay behind, and you are not in a financial position to visit them often enough (at least once a year) and not able to assist them financially when you know that they are struggling.

This brings you to a point of confrontation with your inner self. If you are ill-equipped emotionally, or not yet ready to face defining your feelings and dealing with the truth, you may postpone your feelings. You suppress reality and its effects, and you rationalize your behaviour. You justify to yourself why you deal with the situation in such a way. It becomes a way of coping – even when you know that this coping style is emotionally immature and ineffective.

You are still lingering between contemplating change and that very first phase of pre-contemplation. It may be that you have started to move on, that you have adjusted and almost completed part of the process, but then, when a sudden trauma occurs, it pushes you right back to square one. And you have to start all over again.

This often happens in unsettling circumstances such as having to move house regularly, or facing redundancy – especially if you have financial difficulties together with financial commitments, or you contract a serious illness that impacts on your work performance and therefore, your financial security.

In England, I have seen well-qualified immigrants having to accept 'minor' jobs via job agencies, because the better jobs usually go to the locals, despite anti-discrimination policies. They now work as rubble removers, cleaners, caretakers, and security staff. Many do night shifts for better pay. There are immigrants who have changed their names to something more familiar to the English ear, just to find employment.

To survive in these circumstances, a good sense of humour is one of the bigger emotional assets. You may just have to accept a job that you would never have dreamt of doing back home. Definitely not when you were still back home, sitting in your luxurious chair, in your lovely home. (Or shall we say, the house that was yours, back then?)

The reality of the type of available employment abroad is often a completely different story to what others may have told you. Research by the journalist, Philippe Legrain, indicates at the time of his investigations that one in 10 taxi drivers in New York was non-American and held a doctorate degree or was studying towards one.[6]

When you talk to immigrants in and around London the conversation so easily steers into the direction of their experiences since arrival in the country: those of work, difficulties in finding appropriately paid jobs, adjustment to a lifestyle so different to what they had before leaving their own country, skills and qualifications not being recognized, the yearning that loss brings about...

'It is as if you have no history; they view you as if you were born here the moment you arrive in this country,' said many an immigrant.

Yet, they stay. Often because they believe that it, eventually, would be better here. For many human rights in the UK hold the key to a better future, despite their intense feelings of craving the emotional security that being with loved ones back home, once brought - and a yearning that lingers, as if for ever.

I listened to the sad but courageous life story of Susannah, who I had met on a flight to Doha. She was on her way to Africa where her husband lectured at a, relatively speaking, well-known university. Susannah's story reflects the story of thousands of immigrants who have gone abroad to look for a better life, not found it, and experienced the bitter path of loss and bereavement due to shockingly hard and often sad experiences in the new country.

'London will provide a better income and lifestyle than what we had in Kenya at the time. We thought we could build up a good pension and give our children a future. My husband would complete his PhD in Education at Kings College.' Her eyes shone with admiration for him, even after 15 years.

'But reality struck when he could not find a job to keep us going in that expensive London.' She was staring at Doha's lights far below us, not even hearing the air-hostess instructing us to fasten our seatbelts.

'He was too overqualified, too old, too this and too that', she continued. 'He eventually worked as a security guard somewhere in London, in an old building in desperate need of renovation. It was winter and there was no proper heating. He brought home pennies instead of pounds.

'I was a qualified nurse and had considered taking up a part-time job to help out financially. The children were between ten and thirteen years old, and times were extremely difficult, as neither my husband nor I could find a job. I eventually realized that employers expected me to retrain, which in the end, I did.

'In many ways it was devastating for our whole family, but we persevered. The children are now all qualified here in England and may therefore be lucky to find work anywhere in the world should they need to. Or so we think, isn't it? My husband had gone back home, and I? I have stayed to work for a pension. Then I'll go home too.'

Families are always on the move within their psychological process of change. Within the framework of emigration, the features of this process may hold real, and often, unexpected challenges for the family members. It can be much more intense than it would have been back home. There is so much more to address, mostly within the context of emotional and social isolation – and this can significantly add to rising stress levels.

In any family, wherever they are, members are not at the same level in their own cycles of change. Like in Susannah's case, and also in that of so many others I spoke to. This may lead to inner conflict, ambivalence, and even emotional turmoil when there are major different needs to accommodate and fulfill.

If a member of an otherwise well-adjusted family refuses to adjust to the new, and feels he or she was dragged or forced into the decision to emigrate, the homeostasis of the family's level of psychosocial wellbeing may not only be violated, but become a devastating experience for its members.

This may also impact on the family back home. They are likely to be concerned about their children or siblings abroad, and feel helpless when they hear about problems which they, as parents and siblings cannot help to resolve. This can also be reversed if the family back home start having difficulties and you would have helped was it not for the distance.

Problems usually occur or intensify if the parents or partner do not handle the situation with the necessary unconditional acceptance, understanding and a motivational approach to renew connection and unity.

However, many people successfully come through these challenges, and eventually, when the time is right, they move on to the next phase. You could, too.

Contemplation

It is during the next phase of contemplation that you realize you want to, and should, make the change; however, you still do not do it. This is also a time of preparation. If your emigration lies ahead, you now know that you do want to move to another country. You start to think about the barriers, possibilities, difficulties, and loss that might occur.

It is a time of self-awareness but you are not yet looking at the prospective change in depth, or considering how exactly it will affect you as a person. Or perhaps you are doing so, but still do not have to move forward. You can stay where you are – in a known and comfortable zone.

If you have been living in a new country for some time already, you will find that dealing with the stage of contemplation is quite a big step. By now you realize that you want to adjust well and focus on the present because you know you must. Sometimes, you find yourself thinking that your circumstances in the new country, especially in the long term, may indeed be better for you and your family.

However, this phase still holds inner conflict and ambivalence, and absorbs lots of emotional energy. How shall I say this? It is like passing South Africa House on Trafalgar Square on a bleak winter's day and, as a homesick South African, feeling the flag waving through the emotional deserts and droughts of your ex-pat heart.

But then, if you stand back and look at your journey so far, and accept that you are still on the right track, you realize that there is still a future ahead of you.

You tell yourself that your initial decision to emigrate was not that bad, especially if you and your children are now, physically, in much safer surroundings than in your home country. However, if you are missing your country, and your people, it may still hurt too much.

You wonder when your feelings of guilt will stop, if at all. Is it because you know that your country needs your professional abilities, perhaps more than this new country does? Is it the people from home that you miss? You realize, over and over, that you love your homeland passionately, and that despite your new citizenship, home is where your heart is and your heart is back home.

You fight with these emotions, intensified by an endless yearning every time something reminds you of times back home.

Nevertheless, you begin to acknowledge these feelings to yourself, because they are not going to evaporate into the air. You actively start to deal with the conflict within. You have weighed up the pros and cons and started to make definite decisions. You buy a house, if it is within your means, not only as an investment but as a haven for you and your family. You may even decide to decorate it with trendy furnishings instead of clinging to old stuff that does not fit at all, but you had to hang on to it, just in case.

During this phase, you may experience new motivation and a feeling of rediscovery while you are enjoying certain inner strengths. Allow yourself to become aware of these – indeed, they are there.

Your self-esteem, which might have taken a knock when you were confronted with the recurring demands of change, and accompanying feelings of self-doubt and insecurity, is now starting to show new growth and positive development. You feel that you are slowly heading towards your new or desired goal, because you have actively tried to define it for yourself.

Preparation and commitment

During the phase of preparation and commitment, you actively start to prepare for the change. If you are still in your home country, by now you have accepted that you definitely want to move and committed yourself to this decision – your decision.

You start contacting estate agents to sell your house; you tell your family and friends that you are definitely leaving; and you visit your

53

new country to have a look at the proposed new office, housing, schools, and general environment. You consider your finances and talk to your financial advisor. You talk to the teachers to hear how the prospective change will affect your children. You are indeed prepared to make that change.

Planning is a vital aspect of your preparations. If your plans are not based on a specific and well-outlined financial outlay, you should not go ahead, as vagueness will not provide security. It is a dangerous pitfall, which will, in the long-term absorb your resources – financially, psychologically and socio-economically.

They say money is not everything, but what comes second is actually very far removed from it. Financial considerations play a major role in emigration, and therefore have to be handled with the greatest responsibility, as the consequences of irrational, impulsive and irresponsible decisions will affect not only your life, but that of your family, as well as those family members who are staying behind.

If you have been living in your new country for some time, you may find that you have already started to move on in the process of transitional change. This will be evident in that sudden emotional awareness of a slight feeling of acceptance. For example, when you realize that you have no resistance to certain things you need to do, or when you have to make some new adjustments. You even feel good about yourself when doing so.

'You know what?' I said to a friend during that stage of my transitional change. 'I did not automatically thumb through my South African recipe book when I was asked to bring some bites to a function the other day. I actually thought about what my British friends would like, without feeling like I'm sacrificing a part of my identity, like 'lekker Bobotie' and traditional milk tart, and I didn't sulk because the shops here do not sell guavas to prepare a real good fruit salad, well, not yet.'

While we're talking about cultural entities, let me tell you the story of Heila and her milk tart. Heila is a young South African teacher

54

in London, passionate about her culture, part of which is a milk tart (a soft, delicate tart made from milk and custard, set but not stiff). It is an essential item at any tea party, especially social gatherings at schools and church functions.

During her first few months in England, if the weather permitted (believe me, there are such days, too, and they are beautiful) she used to cycle to school. One day, when there was an event at school, she decided it was time to introduce this specialty to her colleagues. So serious was she about her South African culture that she cycled all the way to school with the milk tart in her rucksack on her back.

Needless to say, by the time she came to present her creation, the milk tart had turned milkshake, or so to say. (Wonder how?) It is at moments like these, that you just know that some of your traditions need to bite the dust, and quick!

Letting go of these types of traditional habits and customs is, however, a small adjustment to make, and will not rock your boat too much at this stage, but you still might not be ready to say goodbye to the old in order to embrace the new. You will be more aware of new opportunities instead of focusing only on your overworked self, and your continuous need for emotional breaks.

You approach the new opportunities and may engage in new change, but often on an experimental basis. You feel safe enough to try something new, and to commit to some of the changes, but you still leave some for later. It is almost if your inner self wants to flick on the yellow light: prepare to go, but please be careful.

In this sense, suppressed feelings of guilt about the changes you have made can still act like an anchor for that psychological elastic string that gives you the scope to move forward, but then suddenly pulls you back to your starting point if you have stretched too far, too soon.

Action

This is a very exciting and rewarding phase of the process of change, because you are actively applying those decisions you made earlier.

You behave and act according to your plans and those previous decisions. Bravely, and with an inner motivation, you experiment with new strategies, and carry out plans and actions, which you have thought through thoroughly.

You start to bond with others in your new environment, as by now, you are ready to open yourself up to the friendliness, but more, the needs of others. Suddenly, you realize that your neighbour's uneasy grin is just the way he looks, even to his family. You start to allow yourself to start reaching out – physically and emotionally.

You start to bond with locals, not only for the sake of your own psychological and mental health, and that of your family, especially your children, but because you are ready to take up a new role in the community: at work, home, church and other forms of community life. At first, it is because you realize that you have to do this, but once you have accepted the process of change and began to adapt to the new, this will come almost naturally.

You are not scared any more of losing your old friends, because by now, you have realized that new friends are an interesting and rewarding addition to your life and having them does not mean losing the old ones. In fact, you accept that your relationship with your old friends (if they are the golden ones), are simply changing face, and it does not mean that you will lose them.

If your relationships and friendships have been built on unconditional love and acceptance, this will not change, however, you still have to keep them alive! The chapter on loss will shed more light on this process.

During the action phase, you will make some emotional investments and if your finances allow, you will buy a house – a big step in a new country. It is a time when your inner voice starts to talk about settling down. You acknowledge to yourself that the present is where you want to be and should be, and you commit yourself totally to its calls. You know that you want to live your life fully in the present, not in your dreams of the past, or in a foggy, distant future.

'It was only after eight years in England that my wife and I could come to the decision to make things work here,' said Gary, a friend of mine. 'After our first Christmas with our family back home, believe me, only after eights years of saving up for airfares for the two of us and our four children, we realized we could not afford any more to hinge between two countries. For years I had lived in the past; not any more. And I will not sulk for being here, not one day longer.

'We are going to retire back home, but it is a long way still. That is why we live and work here now; to save for our retirement. It has taken us a long, long time to reach this stage in our lives, and eventually, we are now living in the presence - as this is where we are.'

I could see the results of their definite decision to make things work: he was more confident in his work, his day to day life, his relationships and his new, active role in his church and work community. He was serious, and has become resourceful and resilient.

Like in Gary's case, you may also find that by now the rewards are starting to come in, especially on an emotional level, as you have regained some self-esteem, which is based on the realization that you are going somewhere with your life. There is a feeling of purpose and direction.

Once you have arrived at this point, you will become more attractive and acceptable to others because of the self-confidence that you project to the outside world. This will make you more approachable for others, as you do not need your defenses like before. You now know that you have what is necessary to succeed in your new environment, which, in fact, has become your 'known' environment: your place. That is how you will now be thinking about it; as 'your place.' You have started to identify with it.

However, if by now, you have realized that your emigration and attempts to settle in a new country were indeed only a temporary phase in your life, and not the end goal in itself, you will accept that your move was not a failure, but rather, a period of active preparation for returning to your country of origin, or moving to another country while you finish off what you still need to complete in the current situation or country.

Once you realize this truth, you will be motivated to actively work on your planned return. This in fact, is also the preparation phase for the process of your return and future resettling back home – a new process, all over again.

How cyclic life can be!

Maintenance

The maintenance phase refers to keeping up your changed attitudes and behaviour, as by now, you have made them part of your life. Therefore, you can continue to work energetically and purposefully on your emotions, and other investments.

In many respects, it can be compared to the successful adoption of a child. Your actions are based on conscious decisions because you want to adopt the child, and you accept that child as your very own, legally and emotionally, despite the fact that he or she was not made by you. Not being made by you is only an initial fact. It is the reality of parenthood with its necessary practicalities and emotional challenges that will contribute to the success of the adoption.

To provide a foundation for a child's successful psychosocial development into adulthood, within a safe and rewarding family setting, is an important basis for normal development and healthy community life. To reach this goal, you never stop on your journey of parenthood; you only pause at certain stages to assess if you are still on the right track, or whether some adjustments need to be made.

In your new country, you also work purposefully towards your pre-set goals. When obstacles arise, and there will be several, you approach them with inner motivation, and, most of the time, by employing the problem-solving techniques, which you had explored previously and found to be successful.

It is not like when you are feeling trapped in circumstances, or crisis situations, where you tend to apply previously successful skills, which, in the new situation, may be inappropriate. In the maintenance stage, most of the time you are comfortable and psychologically free enough not to feel threatened if those previously successful skills are no longer appropriate.

Where necessary, you try to develop new skills and strategies because you have learnt from previous experience, and you trust your abilities and learning style. These new skills and the behaviour that follows from your decision to change becomes part of your everyday life. You adjust to the present and its riveting challenges.

You tend not to sulk any more (not that much, anyway) when the longing for those back home creeps out of nowhere. Having worked hard to build a rewarding new life, by now, you will be able to differentiate between longing for the people and for the place.

You now realize that your previous longing for a specific place, like your old house, might actually have been a longing for the people with whom you shared the place with. It is memories that you cherish, not necessarily an inner desire to be back in that place for other reasons (more about this when we reach the chapter on loss and bereavement.)

If, for example, you discover that your spouse is not happy in the new surroundings or at work, or he/she has problems coming to terms with the changes you have initiated, you now feel emotionally strong enough to trust your judgment and tackle this 'obstacle' or painful experience as an opportunity for growth and development, without risking the relationship.

To acquire such a positive outcome, you will have to depart from an empathetic stand, removed from your own wants, needs and desires, as you should now be ready to deal with what is in front of you. You will have a foundation of regained emotional strength and stability.

If you are emotionally intelligent, you will be sensitive to others, in this case, your spouse's or family's needs, and you will be able to interpret the cues they send out. You feel settled and content within yourself and therefore, able to open up to others. You will objectively weigh up and assess these cues against the current goal and analyse where, how, and if, new adjustments need to be made.

However, it is not (and never should be) a matter of putting your own interests first. An emotionally intelligent person would not do such a thing, and not if you realize that your ambitions have not served the interests of your significant others.

At such a time you will responsibly address the issues with an open mind, and a realistic problem-solving style, willing to look at changes that you will have to make to accommodate their emotional stability. Systems theory says that to serve one will impact on all the others within that system.

In dealing with the challenges of everyday life during the maintenance phase, you will enjoy participating in career and personal development opportunities because you want to give them your all. They are not something that you have to do, but something that you want to do.

To experience the feeling of having settled down emotionally, physically and work-wise is one of the most rewarding experiences you will ever have.

But still, it is important to look slightly deeper into what it is that has made it work for you. What is it that keeps you up and running? What techniques do you apply when obstacles cross your path? Why do your strategies work, or fail?

Exercise 3: *(continue on separate pages if you need to)*

In a freethinking style, write down your immediate answers to the following questions:

(i) What keeps you going and feeling positive? ....

....

....

....

....

....

....

....

....

....

....

....

....

....

(ii) What techniques do you apply when obstacles cross your path? .

....

....

....

....

....

....

....

....

....

....

....

....

....

....

(iii) Why do your strategies work?

....
....
....
....
....
....
....
....
....
....
....
....

(iv) Do they work all the time, and every time? Which ones do?

....
....
....
....
....
....
....
....
....
....
....
....

(v) Identify occasions when they have not worked.

....
....
....
....
....
....

....

....

....

....

....

....

....

(vi) How can you change your strategies into more workable ones?

....

....

....

....

....

....

....

....

....

....

....

....

....

....

....

(vii) How necessary are these changes, and why? ....

....

....

....

....

....

....

....

....

....

If you can answer these questions honestly and genuinely, you may have reached that stage in your cycle of emigrational change where you can safely shed your defenses and your initial wobbly self-esteem. If so, well done! You are not only on the right path in dealing with your changes, but you have been making changes, and you are actively dealing with transition.

Many of the important things that will help you and your family through successful transitional change are, in fact, small things – those which touch on personal experiences and bring with them meaning to life. Not necessarily splendour activities, but things like regular family trips, or other activities of emotional sharing – a time for bonding, over and over again.

You should not only continue with what you have established as part of family life back home, but you have to make extra special effort in the new country, as here it will mean much more to your spouse and child, and will ease their adjustment significantly. Your plans and actions should never be a burden, but you should throw in your whole emotional self, in order to bring about meaning – to them, and therefore to yourself, too.

You must also actively create joyful experiences and time out for yourself. This will significantly help you to deal with stress.

Lapse and relapse

Do not be surprised or shocked if suddenly, you find yourself to be back in a previous stage – confronted once again with the issues of that time. To relapse emotionally is a natural thing and it can happen at any time during the course of transitional change. It happens because there are specific reasons underlying a person's willingness or readiness to maintain the progress that he has made during previous phases in the cycle of change.

Often, there are still issues that have not been fully addressed at a previous stage, and therefore the relapse can act as a red light. It says, 'Stop!' First, you need to look at the old stuff before you can move on.

In most cases, this something is not necessarily defined and, most of the time, the problem is exactly that – the 'issue' or 'problem' has never been defined and therefore cannot be addressed effectively, or at all.

Relapse reverses you to any of the previous stages, even back to the beginning. It therefore becomes an attack on the process of adjustment and healing, in such a way that you completely slide back into a previous phase, away from the positive changes you have already made.

Unspoken fears, anxieties and renewed self-doubt tend to grab the steering wheel and force you to make a further U-turn towards familiar and so-called comfort zones where there are less demands and expectations. (Relapse during the rehabilitation process of a drug addict or alcoholic is a clear example.) You find yourself within a series of demands characterized by that specific previous phase, again.

It is then necessary to assess, analyse and consider again the personal strengths that pulled you through to the previous stage, where you were before you relapsed. It is to look again at those things that you have highlighted in the previous phase before the relapse: things that have added meaning, and the strength that you have found to make things work.

However, it also means that you should acknowledge it: that unexpected and unwanted horror, fear. The fear of success, fear of positive change, fear of an unknown life, and fear to step onto the future path that already lies at your feet.

Is it not that you often feel afraid of a different life or lifestyle, even if it is exactly that lifestyle that you have been dreaming about? Or, feel afraid of a better life or the new person you are about to become? You would rather cling to your current world and ways of being because these are all that you know, even if you dislike them passionately. You stay stuck in the process of recycling, in order to avoid the desired new you.

Transition is not always easy and resistance is often typical of initial reactions to the changes that have started inside you. During the process of emigration and resettlement, relapse to a previous phase could indicate the necessity for a psychological pause. Indeed, it becomes a loud cry for immediate help. When you or a family member relapses, it is not the end of the world. It is simply a signal that you need to look at the inner self again, and you and your loved one's lives in the new surroundings.

The word 'transition' means to change from one form to the other. Realising that, you know that transition needs time to evolve and occur. In your life's journey, this process will take you on a winding road through several green valleys, steep hills, narrow mountain passes, dark caves and tunnels, deep rivers and beautiful landscapes – until you reach your destination and can plant your emotional flag in the solid ground of your newly claimed land.

Therefore relapse can be an area of growth – a time to pause purposefully, and, when you are ready, to pick up and to start again. To slip does not necessarily mean to fall and if you fall, it does not mean you have to remain on the ground.

You indeed will experience stress, but just as much as stress can cunningly crawl into your system, threatening body, soul and mind, it can also be challenging and motivating. How it will be for you, may mainly depend on when and how you decide to use it.

Chapter 5
Stress is a given

Stress and transition: are they a pair?

The researchers Holmes, Rahe and Rahe recognized the significant impact that moving house can have on a person, by including it in their standardized psychological stress scale, which measures the impact of life events at a certain time.[7] More recent research tends to attack this orientation of 'life events', however, if I listen to many of the people I have interviewed, and keeping in mind my own experience as an immigrant, I want to agree with Holmes, Rahe and Rahe.

Their test indicates that moving house is one of the major life events when accompanied by other significant events. Moving to another country would imply just that, as everything changes: your lifestyle, finances, social and work surroundings, roles, school, culture, and much more.

Understanding the significance of stress and peoples' differences in levels of hardiness to it, may explain why some people cope well with emigration and others do not. When you experience high levels of stress during the process of transition, you will find that stress and emigration go hand in hand, as the changes usually occur in every sphere of your life – socially, spiritually, economically and psychologically.

The different styles of coping with stress depend on several factors.

In too many situations, those familiar methods of coping, which have worked previously, all of a sudden lose their effectiveness, flexibility or applicability.

Or, it is a case of high demand and low control, like in a working situation where you have to keep giving, and have no option to exercise some element of control. 'Just do it, or I will report you to your line manager,' is a familiar command in the workplace.

This is something that often happens to immigrants because they just work and work. Why? Because they fear losing their work permits, to suppress their unhappiness, or to survive in a costly country because they have lost so much, if not everything, during their emigration – both materialistically and emotionally. Such a situation may lead you into a state of despair at a time when you actually need all your capabilities and resources to get through the changes and transitions.

At a London symposium in 2008 on the subject of ex-pats in Britain, it was said that research has shown that employers increasingly prefer to employ Poles and other Europeans, because they are almost always buzzing with life, while many Africans appear lazy, and tired on the job.

The reasons for this were not discussed on this occasion, but it appears that people belonging to the latter group are tired because they often have two jobs, are low paid, struggling to survive, and have family back home who are relying on them. They are living in small, over-crowded conditions and are highly stressed. Not to mention having to adjust to a totally different culture and environment. Can you blame them?

This chapter will discuss stress in more detail, because the way you understand it and deal with it also predicts to what extent you will adapt successfully to the changes being made.

Stress is not only bad

Stress does not only have negative connotations. We need a certain level of stress to perform and succeed in our daily activities, physically and mentally. This type of stress is called eu-stress. The right balance of hormonal secretion during this type of stress activates and motivates us to reach our desired performance levels. I know people who thrive on stress, especially in new life settings. It has shaped them, and helped them to move forward.

Unfortunately, this does not happen when stress develops in a negative way. It starts to interfere with our daily functioning, often to such an extent that it becomes destructive and causes mental or physical breakdown. But it is not just those who are under pressure who will become ill, or have a marital, mental or physical breakdown.

Therefore, your success in dealing with stress effectively will eventually depend on how you perceive and manage yourself, your circumstances, and the consequences of your decisions. Your emotional intelligence, which is closely connected to your social and spiritual intelligence, will play a significant role in this regard.

Psycho-Neuro-Immunology: stress and illness

A well-known effect of negative stress is the effect on a person's health. 'Slow down, you are heading for a heart attack,' are not uncommon words in the work place, or at other demanding times in a person's life. A wide variety of stress-provoking events can increase susceptibility to illness. Suppressing the immune system can, for instance, lead or contribute to the development of autoimmune diseases like some forms of arthritis, lupus, respiratory infections, and even cancer.

This has been intensively researched and dealt with in the field of Psycho-Neuro-Immunology (PNI). This branch of Psychology studies the connection and interaction between psychological, neurological and immunological factors in malfunction and disease.

However, research findings are still mixed and some studies suggest that health-related behaviour may be more important than patterns of emotional reactions, although we already know that emotional reactions to adverse events do harm health, and may aggravate existing diseases.

This mostly happens when people are exposed to accumulative, long-term stress, which is often the case when you need to settle down in new surroundings, especially in a culturally strange place. Extensive research on the psychiatric and socio-psychological effects of emigration on the immigrant has been done over the last few years, in several countries. This refers to the role of stress and post-traumatic stress disorder in many of these situations.

Research results are available on the Internet and I highly recommend that you read these articles before you emigrate. Form an idea of what others are going through, even if you feel you cannot identify with them at that stage, that you are different, and your case and motives dissimilar. Informed decisions are always the best ones to make.

What happens in your brain affects your mind, body and prospects

Just like in any new surroundings and circumstances, you will find that in a new country your brain is flooded with additional information, almost all of the time. Your mind is constantly being exposed to incoming messages, which need to be interpreted and categorized so that it can advise you on how to react to them. This process in itself can contribute to stress, as it involves many different cognitive and emotional aspects.

In this regard, Dr Hans Selye, a physician, reached interesting conclusions based on research, which have been confirmed by many others since. He studied stress intensively from 1954 and referred to the concept as 'le stresse.'[8] He recognized that stress causes a condition of shock in the body, and identified three stages in the general adaptation syndrome (GAS), which explains how stress develops, as the body reacts in a physical and psychological way to biological stressors.

These stages are as follows: Alarm, resistance (or adaptation), and exhaustion. If these stages are not dealt with effectively it can lead to Post-Traumatic Stress Disorder (PTSD), which, in addition to its serious symptoms, would obviously interfere with the process of settling down in new circumstances.

Carlson, another expert in the field, found that in the second stage of resistance, the body becomes tired of struggling and starts to adapt to its new surroundings. For a significant number of people however, it is during this phase that the body reacts by sending out all different kinds of symptoms of underlying sickness, and cries out its urgent need for attention and help, to deal with the cause of the problem – the stress that it is experiencing.

It was Walter Cannon, a physiologist, who introduced the word 'stress' to refer to the physiological reaction caused by the perception of adverse or threatening situations.[9] Whatever these approaches entail, these experts all agree on the detrimental effects that stress can have on a person.

In my opinion the word 'stress' is sometimes used too easily, often to escape responsibilities. Unfortunately, those people guilty of such attitudes do not realize how serious a condition negative stress is, as it can lead to psychiatric malfunctioning and severe illness.

No wonder researchers refer to stress as a demon. This demonic picture is reflected in many people, who at some stage, experience the severe impact of uncontrolled stress on their bodies, minds and relationships.

They can tell you that stress crawls into your system and spreads itself all over your body, eventually paralyzing and strangling you from the inside. The paralyzing effect that it can have on a person is reason enough to thoroughly discuss the topic when we talk about relocation.

Understanding stress is a starting point

The extent to which people experience stress will depend on the type of stressors (the source of the stress) that they are confronted with, and also on their personal make-up, their perception of information, and circumstances.

While some people seem to be coping well, it does not mean that they do not experience stress or have never had extreme spells of severe stress during their individual process of transitional change.

Looking at the story of John and Sarah, who moved from South Africa to England, will enable us to identify some of the symptoms and phases of stress, which they have experienced over time – issues that most newcomers to a country will experience.

Before they left South Africa, family and friends pointed out the hardships which might lie ahead of the couple and their two teenage daughters. John and Sarah, however, would not allow negative vibrations to hinder them in their healthy adjustment in England, their new home, for there were meaningful and positive things, which would form the basis of their new life. As a point of departure for their resettling, they bargained on the following:

- Sarah was recruited as a professional to a job where there had been a shortage of UK resident professionals. (Work permits for jobs are only issued if there is a shortage of local people, if it is acknowledged as an essential job, or if an employer can make out an acceptable case along these lines.)

- John, previously a highly qualified and respected specialized project manager, would easily find employment once they were there, as Sarah held the work permit, and therefore he was entitled to a spouse's visa, which enabled him to work.

- This meant that she had a contract with her new employer for the next two years, and they already had indicated that they would renew the contract after the expiry date.

- The recruitment agency dealing with Sarah's case would arrange for their initial accommodation, and would pay for their weekend stay in the hotel upon arrival in the UK.

- The agency also assisted in setting up a contract for housing for the following six months, as the family needed a permanent address in the UK before the British Consulate would issue visas for the spouse and children. Landlords in this country usually prefer six month contracts or longer.

- They were notified of a recommended school for the children, which was within walking distance of their new house.

- With the difference in exchange rates, their financial future looked bright although they realized they would have to make some sacrifices in the beginning.

- Browsing the Internet beforehand, job opportunities in the UK, especially London, were plentiful, and John was not worried about finding work.

Their problems started upon their arrival at there village of destination on the outskirts of London, during a public holiday weekend, or as they say in the UK, a Bank Holiday. They had with them just enough British money for their immediate needs, but when they arrived at the private hotel where they would stay during this first weekend, they were informed that food would not be provided, because the venue was accommodating a function that required the hotel's catering services.

Unfortunately, as John and Sarah had not exchanged their money at the airport, they could hardly afford to buy any food during that long weekend, as their traveler's cheques were not accepted in the shops at this quaint little village, and exchange bureaus in the area were closed.

They were reluctant to use their South African bankcards at quick cash machines because the exchange rate was too high and they wanted to rather hang on to their 'foreign' financial lifeline in the new country: 'You never know what tomorrow might bring.' John had to fight against being distressed. He did not want Sarah or the children to be exposed to his intense worries and concerns about this unknown world.

By the time that they were due to leave the hotel on Monday, the manager was demanding payment on the spot, as the recruitment agency which would have carried the accommodation costs, had not made any arrangements for payment as they had promised initially.

The misunderstanding was only settled late that afternoon. Needless to say how embarrassed they were and, by this time, their stress levels were sky-high.

The house they had been allocated was a second floor maisonette. One of the two bedrooms was the size of one of their old house's two sculleries, with space only for one bed and no side table. This was for the girls to share, and previously, they had been used to their own separate single bedrooms, which in European terms, were double-sized bedrooms.

Opening a bank account was a nightmare and financial credit at shops was only available after two years in the country. In addition, buying a house or car (unless with cash or a guarantor) was only possible after three years of continuous living in the country.

House prices were much more than they imagined and been informed about prior to their move. Consequently, they stressed about the high rent, which they were going to have to pay for years to come, realising that by the time they would be in a position to buy a house, prices would have risen even more. There was nobody at the time who could act as a guarantor, should they be in a position to thinking about buying a house, and they felt too proud to ask for help.

Sarah's first day at work presented the biggest shock because nobody except her new manager knew about her starting day (he did not inform staff in advance about her appointment at the office), and what was more, he was absent when she arrived for their meeting. Later on, she realized that the professional job and the circumstances of the work were rather demoting, and that her professional background would not be utilized in the way she had expected and understood from the people who had initially interviewed her. These people were representatives from the recruitment agency and the new employer, done per video-link.

Although she had several degrees, none of these were recognized in practice, although these were requested (and in that way recognized) when she had applied for the job, and she realized that there would be no professional growth, as she had hoped. In fact, the structure of her new workplace and the company's perception of professionalism and expertise were completely different from Sarah's, and that of her professional background.

Professional development was a priority for Sarah and it was the main reason for her decision to move to England. She thought that they would return to South Africa at a later stage so that she could use her new knowledge to further the South African economy and its people – unless they adjusted well to England, and it was clear that it would serve their interests to stay in the country.

Her work included report-writing, which was pulled apart by some of her colleagues who criticized her English language abilities and her professional attitude. She eventually learnt that the locals tended to approach their work and writing style in individualistic ways, based on their own regional background. She could make peace with that idea, as she tried to accept them within their frameworks of reference. However, it did not diminish the damage to her self-esteem; damage which would accumulate over a continuous and lengthy period of time.

There were also hidden racist feelings towards her as she was seen as a white and therefore capitalistic South African, but these issues could not be addressed or resolved, as no one dared to speak about something so sensitive.

John could not find employment because he was seen as too highly qualified. Yet, places in which his qualifications could be used were not really interested in him. Eventually, he found a job in the security business and started working night shifts, as this meant slightly better pay, but this had a detrimental impact on their home life, as he and Sarah had moved into a new routine of having almost no time together. Their emotional and intimate relationship started to suffer.

Due to the restrictions of her work permit, which lasted two years with a possibility of extension, as well as her contractual responsibilities,

Sarah felt trapped, as she could not resign that easily. The situation was exacerbated by the fact that there was so much that she was trained to do professionally, but not allowed to do because of the restrictions of the work permit. The feeling of entrapment was sometimes unbearable.

Both John's and Sarah's first reaction to their circumstances was to return home, but they were reluctant to reveal their true feelings and thoughts to each other. For Sarah, returning home would mean escaping from a situation that she felt they had been trapped and manipulated into, a position she had never known before. Yet, as the breadwinner, she had to stay put to provide for their needs. In the meantime she saw how her husband's pride was being destroyed by his work, more so every day. She was boiling inside – her feelings of anger and guilt beyond description.

John, on the other hand, realized that it was financially impossible to return home and felt that he had to take charge to make things work. He had his pride to protect, but felt helpless and found it difficult to witness his wife's increasing struggles at work, and her emotional deterioration.

He resorted to his previous disciplined managerial lifestyle, and started to focus on the 'must', 'should' and 'need to.' This freaked Sarah out, as she felt that he was being insensitive to her and their family's feelings, especially the emotional loss they had suffered. She had no energy or resilience left to start working her way through these 'building stones,' as John called his theory.

Every day, Sarah had to face how her fear of professional loss had turned into reality. Her company, true to UK fashion during the first decade of the new millennium, restructured several times, and once again, she realized that she was not being paranoid. She and the other recruits from abroad were merely pawns in the process to provide an ongoing production line during the company's process of transitional change – information that was tactfully kept from her during the recruitment phase, despite her prepared questions during the initial screening interview.

John advised her against taking legal action, as he was afraid that she might lose the case and cloud relationships at work, leading to further financial and emotional strain for them.

Consciously and unconsciously she was fighting with her employer, and the restrictions which prevented her from using her expertise. As this could not be done openly, she suppressed her feelings of anger, bitterness, blame and resentment.

She was scared that she would lose her skills, and felt trapped, demoralized and professionally stuck because she could not enroll on further studies like her colleagues. Educational costs for foreign students in comparison to European Union and local students were immense. Other people could work on their professional development and would pass her on their way – young people in the dawn of their professional lives. She felt that she needed it so much more. Her family had needs, and had suffered a major loss due to this country's misleading recruitment process. Sarah's blame and shame snowballed to such an extent that she forgot that it was they who had decided to emigrate. No one had forced them to.

Despite these difficulties, Sarah found the strength to address her problems and progressed remarkably through the first phase of the transitional process, until one night, when she was assaulted and robbed after work. The experience pushed her right back into the initial stage of stress, and the cycle of change was rudely interrupted.

Meanwhile, John had his own battles to fight and became less emotionally available for Sarah and the children. Kelly, their daughter (15) started a sexual relationship and Rose (13) developed symptoms of anorexia nervosa because being 'fat' was reason enough to be rejected by her peers. Combine this with the pressure of being a foreigner, and you have a recipe for potential disaster.

Sarah knew that her daughters were merely reacting to a difficult family situation and that these were symptoms of deeper underlying issues. They were actually crying out for help. The rest of the family, however, did not see the need for professional intervention and anyway, it would be too costly, so they just carried on as usual, with Sarah feeling even more stressed.

For Sarah there were numerous concerns. She worried about their present circumstances as well as a bleak future with no house of their own, possible old age in a high tower council flat (if they were so lucky), and a life on state benefits if they could ever afford to become British citizens. She heard her ageing parents' unspoken plea for them to return to South Africa, and watched her children grow up without family ties. Put together, they painted a picture of helplessness, hopelessness, and failing parenthood. She watched her husband's self-esteem tumble down: a constant reminder of a situation that was almost out of control.

Sarah increased her working hours despite alarming symptoms of ill health. She had contracted a virus that had weakened her body, but she maintained high productivity in fear of losing extra pay at work.

When she eventually began to struggle to walk, her work duties were adjusted to some degree to accommodate these physical problems. In fact, this added more pressure, as she took on more responsibilities in other areas of work – because she was 'available.' She realized that she contributed to this situation by not being able to say no, but she still bulldozed on in order to finish an already overloaded workload.

Not only did her ill health frighten her, but should she lose the work permit, her family would have to return to South Africa immediately, where nothing was left for them, as they had sold everything they had owned. Her husband was in no position to start again, as the country now had major unemployment problems, and his entrepreneurial abilities had already suffered too much on a psychological level for him to think about starting his own business.

She knew something was seriously wrong with her health, but feared that her work permit would not be renewed in view of the illness and consequent absences from work. In the end, she was diagnosed with myalgic encephalomyelitis (ME or chronic fatigue syndrome), an illness, which had become overwhelming and dictating. By now, she felt that she had no resources left to draw upon, and was exhausted to the bone.

John had also been fighting continuous battles against stress and feared that his known coping strategies, which he had been resorting to, had become insufficient and outdated. The children had their own issues, which are dealt with in the chapter about families.

The thoughts, feelings and behaviour link

From this family's experiences, we can identify several internal and biological processes, which have occurred during the stressful circumstances that they have gone through. As emotional reactions are interlinked with cognitive processes, there are several aspects to identify and understand in order to address such processes.

Looking at John and Sarah, we see how they are moving through the phases of stress. At first it is the fight/flight reaction, followed by consideration and evaluation of possible coping strategies to maintain a known identity, and the feeling of security which accompanies that.

Then, finally, there is the stage of exhaustion. Emotional resources and physical capabilities start to collapse. Accumulative stress over a lengthy and continuous period of time was causing them to head for the pits.

From his research on stress, Carlson identifies three different emotional responses: behavioural, autonomic and hormonal, which are closely linked to the process of stress. These responses contribute to how we address (or do not) the issues facing us, and within the context of this book, during the period of resettlement.[10]

Carlson says that the behavioural component consists of muscular movements that are appropriate to the situation that elicits them. Think about the bull in the Spanish arena, experiencing the threat of the toreador in its territory. It adopts an aggressive posture, growls in a threatening way, and kicks up dust, ready to attack. In many respects, the same thing happens with human beings although these components are mostly masked by certain attitudes and behaviour.

Psychiatrists and neuro-psychologists agree that autonomic responses facilitate the behaviour, and provide quick mobilization of energy for vigorous movement, while the activity of the sympathetic nervous system increases.

Consequently, as in the case of the bull, heart rate increases and the changes in blood vessel size shunt the blood circulation away from the digestive organs towards the muscles.

Hormonal responses reinforce the autonomic responses. The hormones secreted by the adrenal medulla of the brain, epinephrine and norepinephrine (adrenalin) further increase blood flow and cause nutrients in the muscles to be converted into glucose. The brain additionally secretes steroid hormones to provide glucose for the muscles.

Different parts of the brain cause the fight/flight tendency. Integration of these responses is controlled by the amygdala, a tiny part in the brain that is significant for its role in emotional reactions. It directly influences the inter-actional relationship between our thoughts, feelings and behaviour. Daniel Goleman, an expert in emotional intelligence, wrote extensively about its function in maintaining and applying emotional intelligence.[11]

What happens is that the central nucleus of the amygdala receives all forms of information. These come from areas like the primary sensory cortex, association cortex and thalamus, relayed to it by the basolateral group, which projects to the regions of the hypothalamus, midbrain, pons and medulla.

We could say that what you see, hear, smell, taste or feel – all these forms of information – enter the brain to be interpreted and transformed into a message to which you can understand and react to in specific ways. These are the areas of the brain responsible for the expression of the various components of emotional response.

It is, however, important to remember that a person reacts to information with emotional significance, according to the meaning that he attaches to it. It is not the specific stimulus, which causes this reaction, but rather the meaning, which the person adds to the stimulus, which will impact on his or her specific choice of behaviour. That is why people react differently to the same stimulus.

Think about John and Sarah's different reactions to the same situation, when she predicted further difficulties for them based on her perception and experience of their situation, and her feelings about it. John, on the other hand, immediately went for previous coping styles and made use of associative thoughts and feelings, as he suppressed the emotional element attached to the present problematic situation. Instead of acknowledging the emotional content and addressing the level of seriousness, John immediately put forward those coping methods known to him as the only strategy for survival.

Experts in Neuro-Linguistic Programming (NLP) refer to the same concept and accentuate the role, which thoughts and perception play in triggering and maintaining emotional reactions and certain behaviours associated with these.[12]

So, why do we have different types of reaction to stress?

Choosing your reaction strategy

A person's decision to choose certain strategies for problem solving appears to be directly connected to their mental state, which links to a certain area in the brain, the orbito-frontal cortex (part of the cognitive area.) Depending on the type of activity in this area, it can cause sound judgment and appropriate decision making. It can, however, be difficult to apply this knowledge to themselves, and to their personal circumstances.

In highly stressful situations people are therefore often advised not to make major changes in their lives, as these decisions may be emotionally influenced and won't provide a suitable solution. It also may create further stress especially because of the emotional element to it. John and Sarah are an example of this, as they pondered escaping from their stressful circumstances by making an impulsive and immediate decision to return to their country. To change job without knowing what the new one will offer would have been another route for escape, but, in their circumstances, it might have created more difficulties in the long term.

So, why did Sarah become ill? What might have contributed to her illness, or maintained the symptoms?

Prolonged stress

The harmful effects of long-term stress are caused by the autonomic and endocrine responses, which are controlled by the central nucleus. The detrimental effects of stress on health are widely recognized by experts in the field, as people increasingly appear to be developing stress-related illnesses, like some forms of arthritis and diabetes, lupus, heart conditions, and high blood pressure – to name just a few.

Carlson[13] believes that stressful situations increase the release of adrenaline in the hypothalamus, frontal cortex and lateral basal forebrain. He points to research findings indicating that destruction of the noradrenergic axons ascending from the brainstem to the forebrain prevented increased blood pressure normally associated with social isolation stress. This can then affect the thinking process.

He adds that another stress-related hormone, cortisol (gluco-corticoid) has a profound impact on glucose metabolism. Gluco-corticoids break down protein and convert it to glucose, making fats available for energy, increasing blood flow and stimulating behavioural responses – presumably by affecting the brain. Secretion of sex steroid hormones is suppressed.

'Almost every cell in the body contains glucocorticoid receptors, which means that few of them are unaffected by these hormones.' (Carlson, p. 315)

Sex

We learnt earlier that John and Sarah's intimate relationship started to collapse. Under 'normal' circumstances, when this happens in a couple's relationship, it causes different and often, additional problems, which become reciprocal in nature.

When you find yourself in a demanding process of transitional change like that of John and Sarah, sexual difficulties can expand further. At such a time, one or both of you may experience lack or limitation in sex drive.

This lack may become a functional tool to release them from 'expected performance' pressure during a time of severe emotional strain, and having to deal with tiring external stressors.

Were the couple able to discuss their problems openly, and emotionally intelligent enough to be aware of them, honest about the exact emotions that they are experiencing, and able to define these by wording them to each other, they could have discovered a more suitable solution, and consequently, less stress and guilt.

They could, for example, say that although they love and need each other intensely (which they do), and that they are going to take some time out by just being together without any expectation of sexual performance.

Sex and couple therapists will tell you that once a couple relaxes about the subject of sex, nature calls for its own solution and drives them back together sooner than expected. When the stress has subsided a bit, the sex hormones will start to function like before.

However, there is another side to the sexual coin. Some people escape into a hypersexual life and have irresponsible sexual relationships to help them deal with their emotional pain, caused by the emigration and related or other emotional problems.

They are mostly unaware of the psychological reasons that underpin their behaviour, and may find themselves in continuous, unstable relationships, flipping between partners. This often goes hand in hand with a lifestyle of alcohol and drug misuse.

The problem can intensify significantly once children are born from these relationships, especially if one partner wants to move back home, but has to leave behind an unplanned child, creating a single parent family, with its own heartache and pain.

Parenting

Sarah and the girls were spending time together on London's high streets, shopping and enjoying the Christmas lights flickering through the cold, misty afternoon. Four o'clock, and it was pitch dark; a short winter's day shrinking its way into another early winter's night. Crowds shouldered one another intentionally and unintentionally, as they squashed down pavements and subways.

The girls laughed and giggled, losing themselves in the fun of blowing 'clouds' in the cold air, but Sarah dragged herself behind them pretending to be joyful. She was just too tired to enjoy anything and felt absorbed in her homesickness. It was a fifth Christmas for her parents to be alone, and another bleak year for her own family lay ahead, trying to make ends meet.

She knew and understood the girls' need for her emotional presence in their lives, but it was as if she was too exhausted to even scratch together the energy to avail her to them. Naturally, this had led to accumulated feelings of guilt and anger, even bitterness.

She blamed everything which had happened to them, and her inability to provide clear parental guidance to the children, on their move to England: England's expensiveness, its unfriendliness and continuous demands to conform to a microscopic lifestyle for which she had not been prepared. Not in the long term anyway.

Does this sound like typical negative thinking? The type that absorbs you in its vicious cycle of fear, self pity, blame, helplessness and caressing the loss – the type which is recognized as depression with its demoralizing low tides and dark depths, its crying spells and anger outbursts.

Perhaps you think that Sarah has become emotionally unstable, and trapped in her own self-destructive thinking and self-defeating behavioural patterns, which continuously repeat them in a cyclic way – one that she has difficulty escaping from.

Bridges[14] refers to an English historian, Henry Buckle, who grippingly remarked that every new truth that has ever been propounded has, for a time, caused mischief. He states that it has produced discomfort and oftentimes unhappiness, sometimes disturbing social and religious arrangements, and sometimes merely by the disruption of old and cherished association of thoughts; and if the truth is very great as well as very new, the harm is serious.

This opinion appears to apply to Sarah, who seems to have harboured old and precious thoughts, and had extreme difficulty to let go of what was meaningful to her.

The reasons may be manifold, but perhaps it may be that the reasons for most of these thoughts, and the behaviour that had followed, may lie deep within her emotional mind, labeled as unfinished emotional business. Cherished associations and memories safely shelved in her mind were easily available and obtainable for her to reach at, to hold, and to look at, again and again, whenever she felt the need to, as she was pining the feeling of security that she thought these known entities had held for her.

And she became trapped right there – in the active and ongoing process of loss, characterized by the often smothering stress that accompanies it, without having allowed herself time to actively work through the necessary process of bereavement. (The next chapter addresses the impact of emigration loss extensively.)

Acculturative stress

There is also acculturative stress to consider where the stressors originate specifically from the process of immigration. For immigrants to integrate and settle into their new communities in a foreign country, they have to face many factors that can impact on the rate at which this integration and re-adjustment will occur.

John and Sarah's initial life in the UK mirrors several of these factors. There are their expectations and pre-conceived ideas about their new circumstances, and specifically, their pre-planned roles and pre-set goals indicating their dream for high achievements in the new life. These did not work out the way they had expected it to (not soon enough, anyway) and they were left with the deep sense of disillusionment – that hollow feeling of disappointment and not really knowing exactly what it centers on: the specific circumstances, event, or perhaps on the self?

With this come self-doubt, low self-esteem and anxiety when facing social sanctions: 'You're the immigrant, the one taking our jobs and homes and social security...you cannot expect to be part of us...'

There is the distressing experience of discrimination and prejudice against you because you look different, speak differently, wear different type of clothes, or originate from an 'unpopular' country - something Sarah, at times, was directly confronted with.

Many of these factors that immigrants are exposed to, as well as certain reactions thereto may sound obvious, and as if nothing new. Almost as if you want to say: 'So, what did you expect then?'

However, if it were you who have given up so much in the old with the hope to gain much more in the new, and society does not play the game fairly, how would you react?

Post Traumatic Stress Disorder (PTSD): a reality

PTSD is a reaction of intense anxiety following an event that was experienced as having been life threatening by the person and/or having threatened his/her integrity or emotional safety severely, or even all of these. It may often (and usually does) occur some time after the stressful event had happened, and there can be repetitive incidents of such post-event experiences.

It is not everybody exposed to such circumstances that will fall prey to PTSD, but many do indeed. This may depend on the subjective meaning that the person adds to the event, the content and severity of the event itself, the person's specific circumstances and previous traumatic circumstances that he or she had been exposed to, sometimes certain personality traits, and many more.

According to research it appears that PTSD seems to be a 'living construct'. The Internet reports Dr Matthew J. Friedman, executive director of the Department of Veterans Affairs' National Centre for PTSD, who says that it is constantly changing as new information pours in. In the past the victim had to be exposed to an event or events that involved actual or threatened death or serious injury, or a threat to the physical integrity of self or others. The new proposed definition indicates that it is enough if the victim 'learned' that a traumatic event had occurred to a close friend or relative or had experienced 'repeated or extreme exposure to aversive details of the event(s)'.[15]

Many immigrants experience symptoms of PTSD because of the traumatic experience of loss on different levels, the trauma of saying goodbye never to return, and to witness the grief of loved ones due to your actions and decisions whilst being helpless to do anything about it.

Trauma can also occur when you are constantly harassed or bombarded with non-acceptance in the new cultural environment, the knowing that 'you're not good enough, or perceived by others as being a threat for whatever their reasons may be, and if you have to live in ongoing fear of being harassed and targeted by social groups not wanting you in their country, not to mention their immediate environment, the eventual psychological harm can be serious.

Asylum seekers and detainees facing to be deported for having been in the new country illegally, or due to criminal causes disqualifying them to stay in the country, are specifically exposed to high levels of harmful stress and the aftermath of PTSD. Research in this field is active and ongoing, as serious concerns exist amongst psychiatric experts.[16]

Many immigrants are offered the opportunity for therapy to come to terms with the impact of their emigration and their difficulties in settling down in the foreign country. For those who had experienced forced emigration the trauma might have been worse than for those, like John and Sarah, who had chosen to emigrate (more about this in the chapter on Culture Shock).

However, the symptoms would most likely be there and the sooner these are recognized and addressed, the sooner the person will recover and regain the old robust self.

Symptoms of PTSD can vary in intensity and form. The most common ones are repeated dreams or flashbacks, disturbing dreams and traumatic memories of the event, psychological numbing, intense distress when exposed to anything resembling the event, sleeping problems, change in eating patterns, anger outbursts, hyper vigilance, suicidal thoughts, depressed mood with no sense of a future, guilt feelings, a preoccupation with possible threats, avoiding people, events and activities that remind of the stressful experience, physical symptoms like headaches, nausea, pain or irritable bowel syndrome, school or work avoidance, and intense feelings of loss.

In the case of immigration, it is sometimes more difficult to link such symptoms to the process of emigration and settling in the foreign country. Sometimes it only happens some time after the honeymoon phase of life in the new country is over, or when another traumatic incident occurs, which sets off symptoms linked to the initial trauma associated with immigration.

There are so many new experiences and information to absorb and to adjust to, that life can become extremely tiring. Should some of these PTSD symptoms arise, you easily attribute them to physical exhaustion due to your long hours of work, or other demanding responsibilities.

Often you have not really thought about it as being part of the pain of loss experienced so intensely - times when you feel that the pain is physical, as if a part of you is being torn out. And when yearning's clinging cloak covers your morning and your night, your head becomes filled with tears, like a dam waiting for its walls to break down. And you feel that your only hope is that tomorrow will bring along an unexpected opportunity to re-unite with those you love. And even that, so often, fades into the darkness of depression – until bereavement brings with it some wholesome healing and a new tomorrow.

Chapter 6
Loss, grief and bereavement

How can anybody ever understand what you go through when your loved one dies? And if so, how then do you dare to mention grief and bereavement in the same breath as emigration and immigration?

When I talk about the loss, grief and the process of bereavement due to emigration, it is not with disrespect, or that I underestimate the intensity and depth of grief and bereavement caused by death. Rather, I have been so deeply touched by the similar processes and symptoms that people go through when they are exposed to the impact of a loved one's death, and those who are grieving for living loved ones far away, or a past life somewhere on a distant road far behind them.

Similarities in grieving death and emigration

The pain and grief caused by death will always be something that one can never, ever refer to lightly. Such can be the loss suffered once you realize you are in the host country with the likelihood of never returning home again. You realize that you really left your native land intending not to go back, at least not in the near future, and together with that, you realize that the loss involves so much more.

You also realize that grief and the stress of grief are major ingredients of the process of emigration – especially when you find yourself living as an immigrant somewhere else, a concept describing someone else, not you, and yet...

This grief can rip you apart and drain you emotionally far beyond expectation. You discover that grief has more faces to it than you ever imagined – that in many ways it mimics the usual process of grief and bereavement after death, but at the same time adds different features to it. This time, the loss can feel as if it happens over and over again, as if there is no end to it.

This time a person does not die, but the memories of loved ones, who are living thousands of miles away, impossible to reach when you want to or need to, keep lingering in your mind. You are afraid that you will forget them, or that they may forget you. It becomes a physical pain somewhere in your body, which you cannot always pinpoint. It invades your senses, your mind, and your total being. You experience the impact of the stress of loss on a daily basis.

You try to manage it, but it is there – like your shadow, it follows you, leads you, shrinks and lengthens in size, as you feel the sun setting over your past – over and over again. It engulfs you when you see an old woman leaning on what must be her daughter, and you know you are not there for yours.

Or, when you see and hear children playing in the park, realising that your grandchildren will grow up not knowing you any more – not really knowing who you are. Or, that your own children, who now have so many privileges in their new country, will have birthdays and family feasts without their family.

That another Christmas or Ramadan will come and go knowing that your elderly parents, who cannot cope with the cold of the northern winters, will be alone somewhere back home – hopefully with another child who is still in the country. Wherever you look, you search for things that remind you of those back home – and sometimes you even see them – but then realize it was a stranger, just another illusion.

Your grief is intense and it sometimes feels omnipresent. You feel drowned by it, absorbed in its blackness. You do not understand why the positive things about your emigration have turned into negative ones. You struggle to recognize anything good in being abroad, in excelling in your overseas job and studies, or in providing your children with the wonder of dreams. It all has become one dark cloud drifting in very cold air, hanging just above your head.

You fail to recognize your grief as part of the process of loss, because you do not necessarily view your move to the new country as a loss.

Contradicting thoughts and strange behaviour

Then there are the contradicting thoughts. You ask yourself continuously – what about the new experiences, the new work challenges and opportunities? Yes indeed, of course you are thrilled with the new things you have longed for and worked so hard for. However, something within you, which you cannot pinpoint, may stir that excitement – sometimes lightly, other times intensely. It could even result in behavioural changes. You change.

At some point, someone may confront you with your strange and sometimes even troubling actions. Do not be surprised. Looking closer, you realize that these can usually be linked to signs of grief and bereavement. They refer to underlying feelings of continuous or recurrent low mood, little motivation to get started or to finish necessary tasks, little or no satisfaction from things which have usually satisfied you, and feeling sick and blue without explanation.

Reluctance to form new relationships

Furthermore, it can feature in a reluctance to form or nurture new relationships, in withdrawal from others, experiencing crying spells or a continuous lump in your throat, feeling as if you do not know yourself any more, feeling alienated, experiencing sleep and eating disturbances, and losing hope. Or, just not knowing what is wrong, when everything around you appears to be fine. You feel extremely low, and you realize you might be suffering some sort of depression. You do not know anymore, perhaps do not want to know anymore.

What you do know is that your grief is immense. You try your best to keep it from others because you know they will not understand,

and perhaps would consider you to be a pathetic, neurotic soul who cannot get on with life. It can even become an obsession to keep your feelings private, and thereby allowing them to intensify even more. But how intense can it be?

The intensity of grief

Experts say that the intensity of the grief that you may be experiencing will be dependent on the depth of your loss. In turn, this depth of loss will depend on the meaning that you have given to it, or those you know or feel that you have lost by leaving them behind – a measure of love and belonging that you have shared.

Loss has different faces

Then there is also the loss of your previous social and financial status – financial security that perhaps cannot be regained or easily acquired again. The intensity of this type of loss is also determined by the meaning that you have added to its significance in your life at a stage when you still had that security.

Many immigrants will tell you that certain types of financial loss can be, in certain respects, almost as big a loss as the death of a person. The grief is intense, non-stop, and can become a destructive, devastating experience. It is an experience of a downward spiral – nearing the financial and its related emotional pits, faster and faster; and together with that, your identity too.

How you are going to cope with your grief and loss will depend on many factors, which are in many respects, similar to those linked with the process of change, as we discussed in a previous chapter.

When they write about death, experts in grief counselling and therapy agree that it is natural to grieve over death and that it is a necessary process, which people mostly experience and emerge from in a healthy manner.

The same thing appears to happen during the process of adjustment and resettlement in a new country. It is especially apparent during the first phases of this process, which may stretch over years, and mimic, in many ways, the process of loss due to death.

Although your loved ones are not dead, you experience the pain of intense loss especially when you realize you are not going to see them again soon – if ever.

This is aggravated when your financial circumstances, or other situations which you find difficult to control, prevent you from visiting your loved ones regularly – and if for the same reasons, they cannot visit you.

Just as you feel you cannot measure the depth of a loss caused by a loved one's death, you also cannot easily measure the depth of your emotional loss after physical separation from your dear ones, when you move to a country far away.

Of course, you will overcome the influential and intense impact of this process over time when you will be dealing with its different faces as you are moving on, but how it will present or manifest itself in your life is something to prepare yourself for, right from the beginning. And even then, it can sometimes catch you unguarded.

You need to know and understand that what you grieve for is that which has always added meaning to your existence, and in effect, to your life and lifestyle. This stretches beyond the support, love and belonging that you have received from family and friends.

It also includes physical things like a car, house, bank account, work, a specific career and living environment, and eventually, also your culture, which is usually defined geographically, socio-economically and socio-religiously. Not only do you have to accept these losses intellectually, but also on an emotional level, as our inner self tends to interfere with our rational thinking.

It can be hard to acknowledge to yourself that your own decision to emigrate from your comfort zone in your country of origin can also be the source of your emotional grief, financial hardship or other painful experiences in the new country. This is especially true when you have lived a life characterised by financial, social and emotional comfort and fulfilment.

To cope means to understand first

Coping with loss therefore begins by starting with an understanding of the process and the meaning of its ingredients. This understanding should stretch further than cognitive exercises, and should be integrated into your emotions and feelings. It does not serve you well to suppress the reality of your emotional brain's messages and warnings simply because you want to move on as fast as possible, and draw a line behind you, before you are emotionally ready to do so. Unrealistic optimism does no one any good.

You have to acknowledge to yourself that you are indeed grieving a loss, which, in fact, is a process of personal experience – your personal experience. The whole of the process that you go through after the loss, in other words, the way you react to that loss, is called mourning. This mourning is a very important part in the process of healing.

Sometimes it takes a long time to realize that you are really mourning the loss of what you had before you came to the new country. You only experience the feelings and do not always know what to link these to. Or, you guess and link some of your feelings to the comprehensive concept of longing and yearning for home: very real, but also very vague.

It helps to remember that during a transitional phase in life one can identify several aspects, which relate to grieving a loss. It starts with the necessity of realization that when you leave one place to move to the next, you are going to leave behind meaningful entities. These are often entities that you have not really recognized before, but have only accepted as part of your life without realising exactly what they mean to you.

It is like not realising how these entities have served you at specific times in your psychological functioning, and how they have transpired in your performance throughout your life in general. Or, how they have contributed to the values that you hold dear.

The entities can be physical things, like owning a house and often, in the case of relocation to another country, not always having the certainty of owning one in the next country.

This is especially true when your native currency is alarmingly insignificant compared to that of the country of destination, and you do not have a satisfactory income once you are there.

At other times, the loss can be something both social and psychological, but clearly definable, like your previous status, certain relationships which have played significant roles in your personal and working life, or a specific job, which in the new country has the same title but different content. It is during times like these that you often start to realize what exactly it was about your previous role and attachments that has contributed to who you are.

I overheard some immigrants in England saying that it was much easier for the men to adjust to the new life than it had been for their wives. As a woman (I try to be objective now) I can understand this, as many women I have spoken to felt exactly the same. How relieved I was to discover my sisters in motion! No longer did I feel like an island in a fast-flowing European river, but at last, there were others just like me.

Then, when you eventually reach the stage of being able to look back at your process of adjustment, you can even start to allow yourself a little empathetic smile of understanding about your almost selfish clinging to your pain and longing. Now is the time to show yourself some compassion.

I believe that it is the usual association between being a woman and a nurturer that plays such a significant role in a woman's experience of grieving the loss of a past life and family back home. This, however, is not set apart for women only, but can also affect men in very similar ways, depending on personality type and the specific circumstances.

Loss and identity

The concept of loss touches on what you may have perceived as being an important part of your identity at a certain part of your psychological development into adulthood. It hinges on the specific role, which you have carved out for yourself, for example, the role of hostess on a slightly, or a much, bigger scale than six plates on a dinner table.

It refers to entertaining your friends, your husband's work associates, your children's friends and their parents, the hockey club, and in general, being the one who organizes and manages a busy life with meaningful social roles, and emotional bonding, centered on your house.

In South Africa, our social lives involve lots of 'kuier om die braaivleisvuur' (visiting people and chatting away around barbecue fires), even in winter. In general, we mostly lead home-centered lifestyles and children, especially when they are teenagers, are encouraged to entertain their friends at home. Homes are mostly organized in such a way that the children can be on their own without having to cramp up in a bedroom behind a closed door.

Even business dinners are often at the boss's home, or office parties at your home or your colleagues'. Houses, therefore, are usually equipped with entertainment facilities to facilitate this lifestyle, including outdoor life. If you are lucky enough to have your home architecturally designed, it is with emphasis on the entertainment role.

Not to speak of the big role the garden and swimming pool play in this regard! Of course, having sunshine for most of the year accommodates and perhaps even dictates this lifestyle.

When you then move to a colder part of the world, which has small houses and flats as the norm, it can be quite hard because you not only lose the buzz of your social life, you lose much more of that part which has contributed to your identity.

In London, I learnt that people tend to meet in 'places' rather than homes. Yes, they do visit one another and invite friends over, but it appears that the norm for many years has been going to the pub or another public venue (another pub!) as the meeting place. Or they just 'go out.'

For the children, going out costs money. It can be a nervous experience for immigrant parents who do not know the areas where the children go, and have to stretch every single penny.

It can be exciting, but for a previously home-centered parent who already struggles to make a foreign country home, this type of lifestyle can make you feel like your family may fall apart, or that you as a family unit will lose your most precious values. You may feel that you have been let down if your quality of life has changed dramatically for the worse (more of this in the chapter on families.)

I found it quite sad when some immigrants told me that some locals just assumed that they, the immigrants, had to raise their standards to enable them to fit into the new country. In many cases, it was actually a matter of them having had a much better life (financially and otherwise) in their country of origin. But they did not say it out loud, because they felt locals would not believe them, anyway.

The loss stretches further. One could say that it is only the man or woman's loss, but the family as a unit may feel like they are losing some known identity.

Mostly, this goes hand in hand with a significant change in your or your spouse's professional role – especially if your expectations about the new job and position have not been met. Or, when you discover that the picture painted by your new employer and job agency, which has acted as middleman, is far removed from the reality that you discovered once you were in the new job.

Professional loss

It can hit especially hard if you were selected for your specific qualifications and previous job title. Similar to Sarah's shock upon her arrival at her new office in a new country, I have also experienced the essence of disillusionment and disappointment, which required me to redefine and reset my goals.

A British engineer, let's call him Mark, who used to work on a contract in Kenya, echoed my initial feelings of fear of professional loss when he mentioned that he had faced completely different circumstances to what he had thought he would be doing in the new job.

Both he and I realized from the onset just how significant the impact would be on several parts of our professional lives, which, of course, would also affect the security of (in my case) my family, who at that stage depended on me.

Professional loss does not necessarily refer to a loss of status, but indeed, much more than that: it is the fact that you may become deskilled and out of touch with new developments in your actual line of work, of not having access to professional opportunities for growth and development, not being recognized as a professional like you used to be, and knowing that once you are deskilled due to your employer's limited job description, you will find it very hard to return to the level you were at before you left your home country. It is a time of high levels of anxiety and stress, the fear of losing out professionally.

This is quite difficult if you had planned this work as a bridge towards greater excellence in your initial job, which you plan to return to eventually. Suddenly, you have to face the fact that the bridge towards professional growth and development has become a bridge on the U-turn bend, one heading backwards or in certain respects, nowhere.

William Bridges, who has looked at the impact of loss on employees during a company's process of transitional change, emphasizes that people do not resist the changes as much as the losses and endings that they experience, and together with that, the transition itself.[17]

In reaction to this transition, one can become stuck in a certain phase of the transitional process, regress to previous stages, or in a worse case scenario, face a feeling of emotional disintegration (see the chapter on the process of change.)

Your self-knowledge and self-acceptance will play a key role in dealing with such significant change and transition, characterized by its grief and bereavement; especially when you have to embark on the many different types of demands that you are facing in the new country.

Self-knowledge and self-acceptance become significant characteristics, because you are continuously confronted with the way in which your personal management style underpins your success in adapting, conforming and delivering continuously to a satisfactory level in the new surroundings. Actually, in everything else, even in your personal life. Many times you will not even be aware of this.

Allow to grief

The key to not getting stuck in the process of grief, which, in fact, can become an ineffective (but oh so readily available) tool to keep you from such performance, is first of all to allow yourself to grieve. If you do not allow yourself to grieve, you deny yourself the right to grow. Be aware of this because, if you do not grieve, it will catch up with you at a later and often inconvenient time – usually when you least expect it.

You have to accept that when you need to end something as significant as a whole life in your country of birth and belonging, you will be confronted with feelings you would not easily have associated yourself with before, like being very angry, sad, depressed, confused, anxious, disorientated and frightened. Perhaps you previously viewed such feelings and their emotional displays, as a weakness, or as bad morale. They are not. They are all signs of grieving, and their intensity will vary from time to time, even if they are not evident at the beginning.

If you do not acknowledge to yourself that you have these feelings, and cannot name them, you may have difficulty recognizing them in other people, too. This can become problematic in the case of families – not only yours, but also those family members who stayed behind (more of this in the chapter on families.)

Similar to the findings of experts like Worden,[18] Parkes[19] and Kübler-Ross[20] who researched the psychological and social impact of death on individuals and families, writers on transitional management in business settings agree on the consequences that follow on from the loss that their employees experience during the process of transitional change in companies. In this regard, these researchers highlight similar characteristics of the process of grief.[21]

This is also true for those people who have moved to other countries and have to work out a new life away from everything known and dear to them.

During my professional and personal encounters with immigrants in London, I have witnessed and listened to their feelings of grief of which the intensity has fluctuated between months and years. Sometimes just skimming the surface, but in reality, wanting to burst out into flames, and often as an unexpected emotional display.

I have witnessed grief disguised as anger. This type of anger is also seen by several researchers as typical of the first phase of the process of grief, when you often do not realize that you are actually grieving for the past. There is a tendency to direct your anger at others, and at situations outside yourself. It can stretch from grumbling to rage, dragging your feet, making silly and even more serious mistakes, and blaming and shaming.[22]

Sometimes, the anger can be suppressed and consequently, directed inwards, which will lead to low mood and depression. This needs to be differentiated from clinical depression, which has more severe features. Symptoms of the latter have to last for a certain period of time, and are combined with a certain level of social and psychological dysfunction before clinical depression is diagnosed.[23]

It is possible for the grieving immigrant's low mood to gradually develop into a clinical state of depression and, if not addressed, into an ongoing condition. It can also vary in intensity – low, moderate and severe – and this would call for professional help from mental health practitioners. Not because you are going mad, but because you want to regain your self-worth and energy levels. It is essential to seek professional help when the need arises.

Similar to depression, a continuous feeling of sadness despite merry surroundings can linger and if you are not tuned in to your inner language and decide to do something about it, it can almost become a way of life. You cannot reason it away or bury it as a state of non-existence – you can only deal with it.

Susan, a woman in her late thirties, told me that it had taken her a couple of years to overcome her lingering sadness, mostly with the help of increasing socialization with her fellow countrymen in North London, whom she had met at church.

However, I could see the watery shine in her eyes when she talked of the difficult times in the beginning, after the honeymoon phase was over. Especially when she said how she sometimes felt as if she was drifting without direction, even a little bit disorientated.

It is comforting to know that it is not abnormal if you feel like that. Literature confirms that disorganization and disorientation are often reflected in confusion and forgetfulness, the more easily observable things – even if you have always been known as the organized one! You may feel lost and insecure and this can come across as vulnerability, sometimes even as emotional neediness.

I remember a day in London, on my way home, when I, like on every other day, was heading for platform eight at Stratford train station while hundreds of people rushed past me. For a split second, I felt total detachment and alienation. There was not a single known face. It was as if I was walking there for the first time, with thousands of strangers around me. Me: a little island dressed in black like so many of those around me, yet so immigrantly different.

Luckily, the feeling of alienation left as suddenly as it appeared. I think it was because I recognized it as part of the process and immediately started focusing on the reality of the things around me, not lingering on the weirdness of the feeling of alienation.

Actually, it is not that weird at all: it is normal in the circumstances. You cope with it, but if you realize that you perhaps have a difficulty in doing so, consider talking to someone about it. If you have no trustworthy friends at that stage, contact a counselor. Your general practitioner (GP), church, or local newspaper and Yellow Pages telephone directory, or the Internet, should have contact lists of registered practitioners or institutions.

Stages of grief

Elizabeth Kübler-Ross[24] wrote extensively about grief, bereavement and dying. Her research covered different nationalities across borders and has fascinating findings. She said that people tend to experience the pain of loss in very similar ways. Their cultural or religious customs may vary, such as the procedures following funerals, and the accompanying expectations of behaviour from friends or families, but the core of the stages of loss and grief, are strikingly similar.

The order in which they go through the stages are, however, not necessarily the same because grief is a very personal matter. The separate stages of grief can be differentiated but not separated and never fragmentized, just like the stages that we dealt with in the chapter on the cycle of change.

These are most commonly referred to by different experts in grief counseling as being the stage of denial, shock and isolation, followed by anger, bargaining, and depression and finally that of acceptance and letting go.

By bargaining, you try to make sense of it all, however, not always successfully, because it often involves unrealistic attempts to escape from the situation, or making empty and desperate promises. This is different to real problem-solving, and is loaded with emotions, most of the time hidden ones, boiling beneath the surface.

You should not forget that you are still in the process of transition. This transition means you are moving from, moving through, and moving towards. In other words, you are not only going through the changes involved, but experiencing the exclusive elements of these psychological locations: from, through, and towards.

These locations are the entities that have made your life meaningful at that time, and it is these entities that you are leaving behind in order to be able to move on.

You should, however, keep in mind that there will be special entities associated with future locations too, and you need to try and stay focused. Focusing on the future can make things much more bearable in the present. It does not mean that you must deny what you feel in the present. What is more important is how you are going to define for yourself your specific losses.

What exactly is it that you grieve about? Can you pinpoint it, name it, and perhaps when you have looked at these named issues closely, can you reframe them?

Your loss is perhaps not for the house that you once had, but for the life surrounding the family home. Or, not for friends in general, but for the specific role that they had in your life and their contribution to the person you used to be, with whom you felt more at ease with than the current you - this current you, who tends to drift between dreadful, endless longing for those things back home, and the part of you that actually wants to stay and make it work.

Migrants and work permits

For the younger ones, who have working permits for a new country, or for those on short- term work contracts abroad, things are in many respects easier, because they know they will be returning home at some stage, and that there is still a life awaiting them back home. They usually actively try to make the most of their time in the new country because they know it is not going to last for long.

Migrants who settle purely for a period of contract work may have other experiences, such as difficult circumstances back home, to which they have to return to after the contracts have expired, and they usually put in everything they have for the sake of work and pay. Often, for too little money, and many times, abused by employers and job agencies, but they are determined to work and send money home.[25]

I met a public relations officer who works for an international construction firm, who told me how migrants in some firms had been abused financially by some of their recruitment agencies.

Apparently, several of these agencies would attempt to side-step the law by keeping more than what they were entitled to from the migrants' wages, whilst the workers already had received astonishingly little pay.

Despite this, these workers still send the greater part of their salaries to their families back home. Then, there is always the ever-present fear amongst the migrants of losing even these opportunities once the contracts end.

Some foreigners on temporary working permits in Britain experienced the traumatic impact of the global recession when it hit Britain in 2009, and thousands of people lost their jobs when businesses and banks started to collapse. Losing your job means losing your work permit.

Significant numbers of foreigners had to leave the country immediately, as they did not qualify for social benefits, and were also legally restricted from taking up other work, even if it were available.

People who already had permanent leave to remain in the country, the pre-stage to acquiring citizenship, could stay, but once again, they were confronted with the emotional issues of loss. This time it was the status of being unemployed and financially downtrodden, especially as they thought that they had just started to build a life in the new country. Or if, for the first time after months or even years of being unemployed, they had suddenly found a job, only to lose it just as quickly.

In addition to financial issues and related loss, immigrants in many countries also have to deal with the negativity of the locals, who often discriminate against them because of the attitude: 'These immigrants... they steal our jobs.'

In the meantime, it is the immigrants who do the jobs which the locals do not want to do, like working in restaurants and hotels, hospitals, cleaning, construction, labouring, fishing and agricultural industries. They are not always nice jobs, and are mostly low paid, but they dare not complain, as they could be sent home.

You can easily imagine the emotional impact it can have on a person who is constantly reminded that the local people of the country do not really want him or her there, whether overtly or covertly. Self-esteem, which is often already low, can be damaged even further, not to say the feeling of having little choice if a person could not even make it work well enough in his or her own country.

People's perceptions, however, are individual and very personal, and therefore, should be considered empathetically, even when these perceptions do not always reflect reality. To the person, they are real – the grief, hurt and the process of loss are all as painfully real as the world you are living in.

To summarize - bereavement

Bereavement is the reaction to the loss of someone, or something that really mattered to you. This loss can be physical or psychological, and refers to several things like death, emigration, infertility, redundancy, leaving home, degenerative illness, and many more. Grief on the other hand, is the complex emotional response to bereavement, as we have discussed in the previous sections. The process of recovery which is a psychological process is known as mourning.

When you find yourself being acutely aware of what exactly you have lost, and can identify the exact impact of that loss on you, you will be able to recognize the specific feelings linked to the specific loss. It also applies to the specific meaning that that person or that certain something, had (and may still have) for you, and how these have contributed to you being you.

During this time you may have such powerful feelings and experiences that you may feel you are going mad as these can be perceived by others as being irrational, unrealistic and even worrying. Different forms of hallucinations may occur, like seeing, hearing, feeling or smelling the lost person, place or occurrence.

This phase has its function and is not at all abnormal. It provides you with the opportunity, after the numbness has lifted a little bit, to mourn the loss more actively. These often disturbing experiences provide at the same time some feeling of emotional comfort. You see your loved ones who are in fact very far away, or have passed away, and expect them any minute to arrive at your side. You may even lay the table with an extra plate – almost an unconscious act. You see them in a crowd, just to realise it was someone else.

In uncomplicated grief the process of mourning happens over a shorter period than chronically complicated grief, as there are usually more intense, unresolved emotional or psychological factors involved in the latter. This will also lead to stressful prolonged grief.

To overcome your grief and to deal with your yearning, you have to allow yourself the time to grief for as long as it will be necessary. Should it, however, stay unrealistic and become disturbingly irrational, and interferes intrusively in your and your family's day to day lives, you should contact a bereavement counselor or psychologist. This person can guide you sympathetically, but with healthy direction, through your grief towards a wholesome healing.

Then there is the family back home with their similar processes of grief and loss, which are, sadly, often denied or minimized by the family member who has left the country. The same processes that we have dealt with in this chapter, also apply to them.

Chapter 7
Family matters

When family and friends stay behind

You can talk about families in many different ways – philosophically, economically, clinically, demographically, socially and psychologically. But when it comes to emigration, confrontation with your inner self and the essence of your deepest heart speaks louder than any discipline, theory, word or thought. And this is an understatement.

Being an immigrant in a foreign country, far away from your family with little hope of seeing them again (or often enough), the word 'family' becomes alive in its fullest capacity. In some cases, it can become so alive that attempts to desperately smother, bury, or emotionally hide the word fail completely.

It fails because most of the time, people have not dealt sufficiently and effectively with the emotional side of emigration and the processes that underpin the initial change right at the start. Or, they have not thoroughly considered the effect that emigration would have on family members, especially for those left behind.

It is not only the immigrant who yearns for home, the family back home may continue to live the so-called 'myth of return', a myth that some researchers describe as 'the notion that keeps you going, that you are going to be united sooner or later'.

I am convinced that nobody leaving his or her country of origin, will not think about those people who remain behind. My brother, who works in the war-struck Middle East, once said to me: 'You know, I think no one who leaves his country, does not want to return at some stage. They are your people, your lifeline.'

The issue, however, is to what extent do you really give thought to the psychological side of separation before you go, especially during the exciting phase of planning a move abroad?

For many of the family members back home, this separation is forced upon them and therefore the loss is a forced loss, which in several cases, brings along with it feelings of helplessness, emotional devastation, and unwanted change at an unnaturally, inconvenient time in their psychological life cycles.

Often they are confronted with strange feelings that surge intensely through the days and nights that follow. They are feelings stemming from an intense emotional loss, which they had never thought possible, as if the family member who has left is rejecting them. Feelings of rejection run through their being, like a river in flood, dragging with it everything beautiful, and leaving behind a desert of emotional drought and destruction.

Some say that death perhaps would be more acceptable. When a person dies, he or she is gone, never to return. You deal with it in the long-term, and eventually, by grace, you move on.

When your loved one leaves for another country you grieve repeatedly, continuously, over and over. It is as if the mourning does not end, and does not get the chance for completion. You sometimes wonder if it is better not to visit at all, because it hurts all over again after every goodbye.

A couple from Australia told me that at some stage, they almost felt that it would be better not to visit the home country at all. You tend to focus on having to leave again – to see your parents' and siblings' shoulders bent, the tears painfully withheld, streaming the moment they turn around after you have waved them a last goodbye.

And you find yourself tripping easily over a suitcase, because your vision is blurred, too.

Understanding your place in the family setting

To look truthfully at those things that underlie the emotional reactions and experiences of you and your family (close friends fall in this category, too) and in order to deal with these, you have to look much further than just the obvious. You have to understand your own family, and even more, you need to understand your place within it.

It is when you prefer to ignore or evade recognizing the role of your family in your life, and yours in theirs, that there will be an emptiness, which is often difficult to define – an emptiness which may accompany you for a very long time, along the way.

You will just know that it haunts you, and will continue to haunt you until it finds you in that hiding place where you are cringing, armed with thick emotional armoury, hoping that the memories will pass and fade safely into the muddled mist of your emotions. It is like that dense, white mist of a European winter landscape, which preys gently but devastatingly on its victims.

What about you? Have you really considered the impact of emigration on your family and on those who will be left behind? Have you spoken to people who have already had these experiences? Have you browsed the Internet and found those cases of despair? Have you really studied and researched the consequences that your choices may bring?

If you have, then once again you will know that what counts for the one does not necessarily count for the other. Every family deals with its issues in its own unique way. And still research results reveal multiple similarities between the emotional experiences of family members, no matter their background, nature, culture or race.

For years, anthropologists, sociologists, psychologists, social workers, churches and many more have studied family units. It is, however, the impact of family therapy based on systems theory that brings to life many characteristics, patterns and ways of functioning so that one can understand why family members act the way that they do – or react in the way that they prefer to.

Family therapists and social workers will tell you that there are certain developmental characteristics of a family as a unit, but also of every individual part of that family, that predicts to a certain extent the way that they will deal with change. These characteristics seldom move in parallel ways and the phases in which they occur will seldom run concurrently, or smoothly!

Just as a person goes through several, different phases of development during his and her lifetime, so does a family. To fully grasp the impact of change on families, it will be helpful firstly, to look at the psychological phases of human development, and then at those of the family.

Do keep in mind that just like any other cycle of change in human beings, these phases can only be differentiated, not separated or marginalized. They overlap. To move forward often means a step back first, before you can move on.

Emigration and the natural flow of social and emotional development

For the purpose of this book, it is impossible to describe in depth the stages of a person's psychosexual and social development, as the subject is so extensive that books have been written about it in their thousands, over the years.

For our focus on relocation, we shall briefly look at certain significant features during the stages of personal development that underpin many aspects of certain family reactions and functioning – especially when you move to another country.

It therefore highlights these characteristics to show the relationship between successful resettling in a new country and the initial reasons for thoroughly weighing up your decision to emigrate; so that you can consider these before you make the change.

Looking at the different theories of human development, you will find several models, which include the concept of life cycles which are involved in the process of human development, both psychosexually and socio-psychologically.

Do not feel daunted by these. Instead, concentrate on the enlightenment you feel when you realize the necessity of understanding how your reactions, choices and behaviour stem from several features that have existed throughout these developmental phases.

There are the findings of Erik Erikson[26], who wrote extensively about development. He differentiates between several sub-phases of the phases of childhood that eventually, stretch right into adulthood. Other researchers in psychology embroider and add to these developmental theories, describing the different stages of adulthood and that of old age.

Considering these, you may come to the conclusion that moving through your lifespan does not mean driving down a Monaco racecourse, heading for the big reward with perhaps a hassle here or there – a wheel to be replaced, the car filled up with fuel, or loads of expert assistants running to your aid.

The lifecycles and phases in psychological development have a specific function in your life, spaced out and paced, according to your individual circumstances. All of this happens so that you can form an identity, which will carry you through life, contributing to the development of your own seal, which will eventually bring about a sense of uniqueness and wholeness.

The person who has a strong sense of identity is not only the person who knows who he or she is, but also knows where in the life cycle he or she is. To be confident in this realization, there must have been a basis for a strong sense of belonging despite challenging surroundings.

To find the reality, and the sense of a mature identity, you have to complete the developmental tasks, which are characteristic of each of the different developmental phases. Such completion is necessary before you can move on to the next stage of development – just like the phases during the process of change that we discussed earlier.

If not, issues that are not addressed may resurface again at a later stage, and pause or prevent further healthy development. For example, children who have not experienced unconditional parental love in their early years may carry the depth of their experience of rejection into their early adulthood. Because they have problems learning to trust, they may find it difficult to connect with people on a deeper level, which may impact on their future love relationships – not only with a partner, but often also with their own children, and with colleagues and superiors in the workplace.

The theorist, Morris Massey, looks at it from another angle. He differentiates between three major developmental stages, which he calls the imprint period (ages 0 - 7), the modeling period (ages 7 - 14) and the socialization period (ages 14 - 21).

During the imprint period you are the imprint of your parents; a little mould. Their personal and cultural values are part of you, and in many ways you are their photo negative. Put the negative into certain chemicals and an image of the person appears – the parent! It is, however, understandable that during this initial phase, role models will be the people closest to you – your parents and family with their specific cultural ways of thinking and doing.

Some researchers say that certain cultural values are indigenous to the people within their culture. Is this perhaps one of the reasons why people have difficulties in adjusting to or accepting other cultures?

In the meantime, back to Massey.

In the development of values, different things play significant and active roles. As with the different stages, Massey points out that there are usually significant emotional events that shape your values during the stages of development, especially in the first two stages. These events can be traumatic experiences, for example, abuse, death, a significant environmental trauma, or war.

Children who grew up between the 1970s and 1990s in the midst of the bloodthirsty political riots in South Africa's Soweto, Sebokeng, Langa, or Kyalitsha may have completely different values about life and their role from those who lived in the peaceful neighbouring country of Botswana. Or those from violent Baghdad, Basra, or Gaza compared to those who grew up in green British pastures. Draw the circle even tighter: consider children growing up on a London local authority housing estate compared to those who live in the lovely countryside, or leafy suburbs with spacious mansions and charming little houses.

During the modeling years, children start to find role models either inside or outside the family. Having a hero can become more than just admiration in practice. The child may internalize certain characteristics of the outside hero, and may adopt not only that person's attributes, but also his or her behaviour.

If the hero is a negative role model despite being portrayed by the media as the hero, such as certain music and sports idols, serious concerns will arise. In many cases, the role model can be a dangerous community leader or gang member. In these scenarios the parents will need a subtle but firm approach in mobilizing acceptable and pro-social persuasion, and methods of re-influencing their child for the better.

To do this does not always come easy. Britain's recent problems with escalating youth crime and violence are an example of this. Gangs (yobs) are comprised of individuals seeking to be accepted and admired by their peers, to belong and to be recognized. They go to extensive lengths with antisocial behaviour just to belong somewhere. Youth workers and probation officers will tell you how intense the issues of identity confusion can be amongst these youngsters, who are often as young as nine and ten.

During this molding time in the youngsters' lives, their need for belonging and being part of a crowd (even if the crowd totals only three or four) can be overwhelming. Through the psychological process of identification with the peer group, and its actions and values, they gradually form an identity – even if it is a twisted one.

Therefore, positive parent-child relationships during the forming years are extremely important. It provides an emotionally and socially secure environment in which the child can develop. You will know that one of the most important prerequisites for positive parent-child relationships is to try to understand your child, and not judging him or her. It stretches much further. It asks for parental love practiced actively by the guidance that you provide to your child, based on knowledge and set goals. It is love within set boundaries.

Boundaries, if motivated by responsible love, provide security, especially during the formative years of the child.

When children reach the so-called socialization period, they are close to and mostly in their teenage years; those passionate years of *Sturm und Drang*, of up and down the emotional ladder, living to the full, falling to the full, and feeling to the full. It is a time when the peer group plays a significant role, perhaps more than in any other time of life. Within the peer-group they are continuously exposed to new ideas through the people, especially peers, with whom they mix. And they deeply want to be accepted, to be acknowledged and to be recognized for being part of a group.

During the socialization period, which Massey says continues to around 21 years of age, the person is in the process of integrating values, norms and beliefs more fully into their personality. From this, he eventually develops his own identity. When looking back one day, he will then find that the major influences in his life have been friends, educational figures, media, work, leisure, religion, culture, politics, family, and art – name it and it will be there.

I remember parents from different cultural backgrounds, although most of them had similarly conservative values. How shocked they were upon arrival in their new country, when confronted with so-called questionable morals and values, compared to their perceived conservative countries in places like the Middle East and Africa.

'To see your daughters, who used to wear clothes covering more than just the necessary, all of a sudden dressed in ultra-mini skirts, trousers clinging desperately to hipbones, bra-like tops and hair all the colours of the rainbow - not to speak of the studs and rings hanging from every lobe and opening', a parent remarked with eyes rolling heavenwards. 'I tell you, this can be more than just an emotional shake-up.'

Then there is the business persona, which usually occurs between ages 21 to 35. It is said that when it comes to work ethics, your first employers and the people you work with are the people who may have the biggest impact on your ethics. You could say that your values, internalized during your developmental phases, create your reality. They will determine the game you are playing and the rules you play by. This would explain why age, personality and work circumstances are of the utmost importance when choosing a career. Especially if you are starting that career in another country or culture which has different values to your own.

Reality in such a context would mean your subjective reality, and your own, subjective truth. This truth does not mean the truth or the reality of the world around or outside you. It is a truth that comes from inside – stemming from how you have filtered information from outside into and through your mind, and to act from this subjective departing place.

No matter what age, every individual in a family is, at the time of his or her emigration, in a specific phase of social and psychological development. This will continue in the new country. How it will develop further depends not only on the natural process and flow of development according to age, but also on environmental and other influences. However, it will mostly be born from the person's own perceptions and experiences in that country.

Parents who want to emigrate will therefore have to attend specifically to their children's and extended families' natures, character, emotional strengths and weaknesses, or in short, their psychological hardiness, and also, their interpretation of events at that stage.

The extent to which these aspects matter to you as a parent will, in effect, impact on how your child will view family life, and subsequently, the significance and meaning that he will add to a family member's place in the family. It is by the way that you have educated your child about their understanding of their own feelings of emotional belonging (or not) in your immediate nuclear family, and how you understand yours regarding your family back home, that they will eventually understand their role in this wider, extended family. Parents, therefore, set the example when it comes to family life and inclusion or exclusion of the wider family.

If you live mountains or oceans apart from one another, with little and no contact, you as a parent have to work much harder to keep the bond alive, to instill in the child the knowledge that the wider family is still out there, that they need one another, and need you. This does become difficult if families and friends do not value attempts and specific actions for contact important enough, and do not realize and accept their emotional duty towards one another. Your child (and you) could then react with intense feelings of rejection and disillusionment. 'They do not contact me anymore, so why shall I?' But you need to continue to persevere; that is to say, if the family or friend is a morally healthy one!

There are, sadly, situations where it would be in the interest of some individuals and families to start a life away and disconnected from their family of origin. Usually this would be in the case where harmful relationships, negative influences, and extreme dysfunction have prevailed and the victims of these, need to build a new life, and for them, a new identity.

Your example of being realistic about the way you keep alive family values, meeting emotional needs, and in developing healthy emotional hardiness to deal with these issues, stays a crucial factor. You can reason that this may be the basis from which your children have formed their definition of what a family is, and what they can expect from family life. This definition is therefore based in their perception and consequential expectations.

Of course, these perceptions can change and in many circumstances will change, however, it will not happen that easily; and when it does, it does not happen without emotional discomfort. How you plan to deal with this is the secret to successful transitional change in your personal life, and by way of its rippling effect, in your family's life, too.

When referring to the different stages of adulthood, psychologists talk about the challenges and characteristics of the different phases. Mid-life is such a stage when you start to look back and evaluate your life: 'where am I?', 'where am I heading?', 'are all of these things worthwhile?', 'what is left for me?'

This is also the time when, as you look at your family of origin, you see that roles start to change in many, significant ways. Amongst other things, you may slowly be heading for the role of carer of your elderly parents as they age. This can take on many forms. Having to face a new role of being your parents' carer may bring new demands and conflicts.

There is the expectation of having to fulfill this role, and at the same time, having to actively continue in your role as mother or father in your own home, with all the responsibilities and demands that this holds. You may now find that you have conflicting roles and responsibilities – your husband or wife, and children, on the one hand, and your ageing parents, on the other.

If this process happens all the time in family life in natural circumstances, just imagine the impact that it would have on a family who has loved ones far away in another country. It can become immensely difficult, and even heartbreaking, for the child who is abroad to deal with the fact that he or she cannot be there for the ageing parents back home.

It is therefore essential that you know, understand, and also ack-nowledge your own character, personality and family values before you emigrate. You and your family should discuss the family's expectations in this regard, especially if it is likely that you might not return home.

When the reality of old age and the death of an elderly parent creep closer and closer, it may become a suffocating experience. Therefore, you should be aware of the power of your emotions. Be careful not to allow them to override cognition in these difficult times. It is often during such emotional times that feelings of conflict intensify and illuminate those issues of the past, which perhaps were not dealt with satisfactorily at the time.

In some cases, it may refer to not having cut the apron strings when it was necessary during earlier development phases, or guilt trips that parents had played on their developing children in earlier years due to their (the parents') own psychological baggage and unfinished emotional business at the time.

The person who has been brought up to be the responsible carer of his or her siblings, together with a set role imprinted in his or her mind defining him or her as carer to the elderly parents, will most certainly be exposed to continuous feelings of being torn and psychologically dissected when he or she is not readily available during these later years.

This may also happen in families where there are no lingering issues, no mutual hurt and no unrealistic expectations. In fact, it can happen anytime to anyone that has been part of a loving family.

Do you know just how hard it is to leave an elderly parent behind at the end of every (hopefully at least annual) visit, to see how much he or she has aged the next time you return, to hug him or her goodbye and wonder if this will be the last time. And for some time afterwards, you may wonder if your emigration has really been worth it.

It is during times like these that you need to keep your head straight and to acknowledge this cognitive dissonance as being natural in the circumstances. It can last moments, or months, even years - much longer than you initially had prepared for.

Cognitive dissonance is more than that startling awareness of psychological conflict. It can set off anxiety, which may engulf you with its intensity, and which, in these circumstances may forcefully roll over you as waves of worrying and renewed doubt, making you feel as if you are going 'to lose it.'

You may feel tempted to make impulsive and highly emotional decisions, such as leaving everything in the new country and returning home immediately. You know that this stems directly from your beliefs and attitudes, which have been present simultaneously – therefore there is conflict within you.

As before, at such a point, you should again start weighing up the positives and negatives of your life journey. If the cons are greater than the pros and you know that in your family, togetherness in old age is the most important thing to ensure a peaceful life ahead for all of you, you may then wish to consider returning to your home country.

When aged parents are kept under the impression that you will return and you choose to postpone your return without a valid reason, it could, understandably, become too much for them to bear. They may lose hope and trust and that could have a devastating impact on them at this stage of their lives.

What if it has become financially impossible and, in certain circumstances, unwise for you and your nuclear family to return home? Then you must accept it, although it is hard, and you must let your parents know this, too, which can be even harder. Remember, for any loving parent, his child's financial security is highly important and provides the emotional assurance that 'my child will be okay,' especially in today's expensive living climates.

However, it is not easy.

When old age starts to slip in and you have accepted that your grown-up children are responsible for taking charge of their own lives, you, as the elderly parent, can look back on a fulfilled life characterized by realistic expectations. You can still enjoy feeling content with the knowledge that you have succeeded in adapting to changed circumstances, even the unexpected and unwelcome ones. You can enjoy having more time on hand to continue your spiritual development. You know that your children are cared for, safe, and still love you, like always.

You thank God for guiding you through those valleys of life, where you have taken advantage of the opportunities given, to contribute to your children's success and progress, as well as to life's greater needs.

If you, the elderly parent, have not invested in a meaningful life and have found life's struggles too much to bear, because your level of emotional hardiness has not always served you well, you may, unfortunately, be confronted (again) with issues of an identity crisis at this stage in your life – and consequently, experience feelings of despair. If it becomes too difficult, do consider seeking professional help from a psychologist, specialist counselor or psychotherapist, or a well-qualified life coach.

You too have to reassess the quality of your relationships – it is never too late to work on these. Development does not stop when you turn twenty one or forty. It continues until the end of your life. Looking at it from a spiritual point of view, it actually stretches beyond the earthly life that we know now. Are you not, perhaps, preparing to meet God, and therefore working on developing your spirituality in order to connect with Him?

In order to have a meaningful life in old age when your children are abroad, you have to maintain the focus on the importance of cherishing and nurturing friendships, starting new ones continuously (although this is not always easy) and enjoying bonding with your children. Bonding which of course will be different now than in earlier years, when they were still your dependants, or when they were living nearby.

This is also true in the case of the older immigrant who finds himself suddenly alone in the adopted country when his children have left for yet another country. He or she can feel that it is too late to return home to the homeland, and too late and out of rhythm to go after the children to a new country - and thereby, should they do so, repeat the whole cycle all over again.

Remember we said earlier, that we tend to look at life through the filters of our minds, and thereby make an event or situation into what we want it to be – something that mimics a previous experience?

The circumstances described above may result in separating reality and emotions to such an extent that in this case, struggling with the emotional side and its impact may wholly absorb you. That is if you do not stay in control of your friendships when the children leave.

You may find it extremely hard to focus on reality when it becomes intertwined with the unsettling emotions that have accumulated over the years, which are now about to erupt like a bottleneck with a shaking lid, screaming to be blown off.

This would be an appropriate time to seek that professional counseling or therapy that you have already thought about unconsciously, and therefore learn to deal with the separation successfully. You will then be able to continue your life in a meaningful way. You have to.

You can still be the strong pillar behind the child who has left the country. Remember, they have not left you, they have left the country. You will always be in their minds and prayers – just as they are in yours.

There is nothing stronger than a healthy emotional bond between people who love one another. This will also form the basis of that inner strength, which enables both sides of the family – parents and children – to deal with any issues in the future that require emotional determination and perseverance. You will need it when you are establishing this new part of a changed life – 'you' in the new country, and 'you' who stayed behind.

With this, I do not minimize the emotional impact of such change. On the contrary. I have witnessed many tears, and have shed my own, but there have also been smiles of realistic hope and the peace that acceptance brings with it.

Sadly, there are also those cases where separation has become a central theme in a person's life, as well as in that of a family's.

An immigrant from Kosovo told me the heartbreaking story of having to face deportation after nine years of living in London legally, as an asylum seeker, after the wars and hardship in Kosovo. Having settled in the UK, he found a girl with whom he madly fell in love, and after four years together, they have had a baby. By this time the baby was three years old. She had her father's black, curly hair and her mother's sensitive blue eyes.

But he committed a crime: a mistake born from financial need and illogical ways of solving problems. He served a lengthy period of imprisonment for the crime. Now, he is awaiting the final decision of the immigration board. It is highly likely that he, despite his plights and application to stay based on human grounds, will be deported because of his crime. Should he be deported, his partner and daughter would have to stay behind. He feels he cannot expose them to a devastated country from which he had initially fled in search of safety and security. Should they eventually decide to accompany him, it would be them who might become the victims of immigration, as he viewed himself to have been in England.

By the time of my intervention in his life, the blame and shame of the extended families had become immense, and by that stage, everybody in the family had suffered, as they had all experienced the devastation that forced separation had inflicted on them.

Challenges of family life abroad

When we delve deeper into the challenges of family life, interesting features emerge. These features will eventually ensure the ebb and flow of the family's life through its different life cycles, and therefore the different cycles of change.

Systems theory tells of members of a social unit, their role and function within this unit, the unit's structure and unique components with its attempts to bring itself to a state of maintained equilibrium.

Therefore, the pressure on its members to fit in and to perform in accordance with its own norms and values can become a major challenge (and issue) faced by families separated by emigration, because the family has always been the prime social unit in society. The many forms of 'family' in different cultures do not matter as the basics stay the same.

The nuclear family (father, mother and children) is seen as the most important unit in social existence, as it forms the basis for the child's healthy development – physically, emotionally and socially. From here, he will reach towards the outside world to learn about it, knowing that he can return to the safe base of unconditional family acceptance and support, try again, and eventually, be ready to leave the nest.

His parents provide that sense of security for him. They know that their child exercises and tests his growing and developing potential in this safe space. He learns about the importance of relationships and builds the confidence to embark upon successful independence.

As the parents witness and allow this development in an empowering and supportive way, they know that this is also their emotional investment in the child, as that child will value them enough to maintain a meaningful relationship in the future, wherever he or she may be living.

We must understand and accept that when major changes occur in the family, it affects everybody in that system. There may be members in a family who, against all odds, may want to prevent the change from occurring. Or a member may desperately try to mend what he or she has interpreted as being broken, or perceived as being emotionally too threatening to allow it to continue.

There are those families who eagerly cling to their previous roles within their family system attempting to save old structures and thereby intensifying blurred boundaries. These boundaries refer to the necessity of psychological or emotional privacy for each family member within the role that he or she has in that family unit. This may be, amongst others, the role of parent, father, child, or sister – or parents, and siblings.

Clinging to outdated roles or functions, or having difficulties with boundaries, can be a problem in any family. However, it may impact further on those families who are separated by emigration. Often the families who leave for another country have little or no chance left to address the loose ends of those issues that have not been dealt with. These issues still linger, long after the plane has departed.

It may be easier for those living closer to their countries of origin, who can perhaps visit more regularly, and have more opportunities to address the emotional issues that have arisen as a result of their emigration.

Airfares between these countries are cheaper most of the time. As a European citizen, for example, at this stage, you do not need visas in addition to a passport, to travel all over Europe, the Balkan countries and the United Kingdom. Transport is not as expensive as it is to go to Australia and Africa, especially South Africa. And if you live 'east and west' apart, and need more than one flight connection, it can be a tiring, and difficult financial experience.

'We did not realize when we left Namibia that it would continue to be beyond our means to go home for Christmas. We have four children. Airfares are just too much,' said the woman at the other side of my desk.

I know. I'm South African, I thought, but I did not voice it. I also did not say that having one child does not necessarily create a better picture.

Then there is the Zimbabwean girl with sad, misty eyes: 'My mother usually comes to visit in October when it is slightly cheaper than December. We have an early Christmas. I want my son to experience something of family life when it is Christmas. You know, I never realized that I would not be able to afford tickets for both of us over Christmas. Prices are double this time of year.'

Dealing with long-distance relationships

Being honest with yourself will always be one of the most important things in your life. In the context of emigration, you should be scrupulously honest and upfront about your and your family's financial status, as finances (mostly) will dictate the frequency with which you see one another. It is these opportunities to be together, which will eventually shape the long-distance relationship.

If your family back home cannot afford to visit you, and you cannot go there regularly, you have to admit to yourself and accept that your decision to emigrate will bring permanent changes in the way in which your relationships will develop. They may even become estranged, and eventually disconnected.

You may even become unrealistic, and create for yourself a fantasy world to cushion your grief. As time moves on and you start feeling increasingly guilty and alone, you may start to idealize your family of origin, until you picture such a beautiful family setting that you start 'living' it in your mind's theater.

To idealize your family of origin is a very natural thing to do. However, you can become so absorbed in your daydreaming about that family, that you can be left with very little emotional energy and time for your present family, who is fighting for your attention and closeness.

As you live on in your dream world, you may increasingly have problems finding sufficient emotional resources within yourself. (Remember Sarah's case in a previous chapter?) And when you decide to return home permanently to be close to your family 'all for their sake' (or is it yours, in fact?), something extremely sad, but real, may happen: you could be confronted with intense shock.

You may realize how wrong you have been: that this wonderful warm and flawless family that you have been dreaming about, or have created in your mind, is just ordinary people - flesh and blood like you.

In some cases there are also those families or family members who are impregnated with the emotional scars of many of life's demands and unresolved issues – and you only realize it now. Like Mary, a British-American woman who told me about her emotional devastation when she discovered that her parents had turned into alcoholics during her absence. The real picture of her family was far removed from the memories that she had cherished and the cozy family picture that she had created in her mind during their time of separation.

It took Mary a long time to come to terms with this. She eventually decided to leave England, this time for good. At the time of our interview, she was preparing her return to America.

'I'm going back to my friends. I realize only now that they have been my family all the time. Do you agree, family can be something you create, and not necessarily by your flesh and blood? I think the creation of a family in these circumstances is something stemming from need: the need for belonging, for recognition, for unconditional love and for togetherness…

'I think it is all about people. People you can relate to, with whom you share interests and emotional heritage. Something like a spiritual bond between you and them – because you have learnt to trust again, to trust them. You know they accept you for who you are. And you know: there where you think you have found these, there you build your emotional home.'

Does Mary's voice not mirror the thoughts of perhaps many more immigrants all over the world? Does her parents' downhill spiral highlight the difficulties facing by many people who stay behind and who find it very hard to come to terms with the additional weight of emigration loss?

Similarly, there may be parents back home who are disappointed to see that their loving child has grown into an adult with his or her own way of thinking, attitudes, and life, often very different to theirs. Or has become an adult with changed norms and values; to the parents often unacceptable – a person they would not have liked were he or she not their child.

To maintain good and meaningful relationships you have to accept responsibility in finding ways to do so. You need to stay in contact to maintain the bonding, the love and the care. It is too easy to drift apart should you not keep contact in a meaningful way. You know that distance prevents you from regular physical contact; therefore you need to think creatively. What has been important and meaningful to your loved ones in the past? Can you continue with these? Does meaningful mean to them something different than what it means to you? Is it perhaps letters instead of e-mails, paper photographs instead of emailed photographs, telephone calls and internet imaged contacts? Do you keep in mind that maybe your elderly family and friends abroad are not that familiar with technology; that they are uncomfortable to use a computer, but too embarrassed to say that?

If you do not contact one another enough in a meaningful way, it is easy to drift apart and damage the quality of the bonding, which was there before.

To stay realistic about your roots and the people back home, you have to maintain emotional sobriety and have constructive contact. Just to continue dreaming about visiting 'next year' and not do anything about it, will not help you one bit. If you do not make specific financial plans to materialize your dream, and make it a priority, you will keep postponing it and it will remain a dream.

In such a case, your inner feelings of guilt will continue to flourish and you may expose yourself to the anger and blame of your family members who may start to think that you do not really care about them.

It is difficult for the family back home to understand that you have a paid job with the benefit of leave, but you never come to see them. To tell them year after year, 'I cannot come this year', is not good enough. You have to be honest with them. Tell them in an acceptable, sensitive way, why you cannot come and that you are trying to find the means to do so. Continue to reassure them of your love and commitment.

Then keep to your budget, explore ways of earning extra money to finance the trip, and put your shoulder to the wheel. Do that extra job and save the money for that specific purpose. If you have difficulties with the discipline of saving money, arrange a direct debit to your savings account, even if it is only a small amount. Buy your plane ticket in advance when it is cheaper, or when the currency is more favourable than usual.

This sounds so obvious, you may say. Yes, it is obvious. However, when things become difficult financially, or when you get so tied up in your work commitments or studies, postponing can become the main ingredient in your lifestyle in the new country.

Often, it can be a characteristic of a person's way of functioning. He or she is always postponing things in order to avoid taking responsibility. Is it not, in such a case, a matter of avoiding self-honesty and sidestepping acceptance of the consequences of your initial decision to emigrate?

This will not serve you or your family back home, well. Instead, you are hammering the nails into the relationship coffin, one by one, whilst axing your own psychological progress and development. It could become a self-defeating behavioural pattern, where you might have difficulties breaking away from such a cycle of continuous self-defeat.

For the person who tends to be a worrier, stingy and always over-whelmed by the feeling of being in financial trouble, it can even be harder. His or her focus stays on the self-claimed unsatisfactory financial position, in which, psychologically, he or she will eventually drown.

This is not to deny that many people have financial troubles, and are forced to stretch their pounds and pennies. It refers to those who lose sight of the bigger picture, psychologically. Many habitual worriers and inefficient prioritizers find that they are indeed financially able to continue with a life filled with habitual spending. They buy a lunch pack every day, sit down regularly at a street café and enjoy a quick sandwich and coffee, go to the cinema and theatre regularly and religiously buy the accompanying Coke and popcorn, or pre-show sherry, just for the sake of it. They dine out twice or thrice a month.

These are the small pleasures in life, so they say, the not-so-costly ones. However, if you start counting such spending in one year, it could easily total the price of a plane ticket home.

Or they say they cannot afford to buy the relatively expensive £600 plane ticket to visit their family, but for two or more consecutive years they religiously (again) go on their usual holidays, which easily adds up to the same amount as the plane ticket, if not more.

In many circumstances, prioritizing means making sacrifices. And perhaps you have now reached a time in your life when you realize that your family and their emotional wellbeing is a priority. Admit this to yourself, plan ahead, strategize, and work actively and purposely towards your goals.

Keep to your plans, and before you know it, you will be standing at the airport once again for that much needed visit, passport in the one hand, ticket in the other.

Use your creative mind to find ways of sharing experiences with those back home. Read the same books (try to), watch the same films and sports events on television and discuss them over the phone.

Send regular text messages, letters or emails filled with love and care. Computer games, which have worldwide participants, offer a fun-filled experience of togetherness, even though you are not physically together. Invest in electronic exercise games and master the techniques together – especially if there are children in the family.

Think of making your own Christmas tree decorations, which represent absent family members. You can use individual photographs of family members to decorate the Christmas tree. Children can be amazingly creative. Pick up on their ideas.

Or create other rituals in line with your traditional customs and beliefs to commemorate your loved ones. In this way, you bring your absent family members (and close friends) into your home during these special times.

This can contribute to ways of keeping your children's ties with those back home, alive.

Hidden issues

Unfortunately, there are sometimes hidden issues in couples' and families' lives, which can hinder or obstruct a member's attempts to maintain significant contact with the family abroad. This could interrupt successful adjustment to the changed circumstances significantly and may also affect one's coping strategies in several ways. Often the owner of the hidden issue is not aware of this as it lies in the subconscious, or even nestles deep in the unconscious mind.

This brings about inner conflict and stress. We have already learned how stress can accumulate over time. In situations where relationship and related communication problems exist, stress levels can increase alarmingly, with a tempo and intensity you hardly can imagine.

Having worked therapeutically with couples and families in crisis, I found what so many other counselors and family therapists have discovered too: Friction between partners does not arise for the first time in the new or changed situations, and it does not develop in these circumstances, from scratch. It has been there all the time, or at least the seeds were already sown early in the relationship. They just needed the right environment and climate to bud and grow in.

The process of emigration and resettling in a new country can easily be this environment, and situations in the latter can trigger old wounds to start bleeding again, suppressed issues in the relationship to become alive and unresolved issues to spring up again – all of which are disguised as new ones.

Just as having another baby does not resolve a fickle marriage, moving to another country to start afresh will not solve relationship problems.

In fact, it will accentuate, increase and magnify existing ones and eventually drive you apart, even further than you were before.

If you and your partner have problems communicating meaningfully, this may become even more difficult when you are confronted with the emotional challenges of emigration, and having to deal with your adjustment issues in the new situation.

Your emotional journey through your own process of loss, often characterized by painful struggles, may cause you to appear to your partner as a very different person to the one that he or she had known before.

How the partner chooses to interpret the other's behaviour and attitude is mostly embedded in his or her subjective viewpoint based on previous experiences, as mentioned before. The person may appear to be cold, unapproachable, distanced, withdrawn, difficult, dangerous, or pathetic.

None of these interpretations help when it comes to dealing with the issues confronting you. However, they can be the only familiar thing to the observing partner, who only knows his own feelings about the other. He may then often cling to these feelings because they are all that he knows, even if they are destructive and unacceptable.

If you have a partner who has no or little understanding and patience with someone struggling through difficulties, or who has always had objections to acknowledging his emotions, who has no time for failure, and who always expects delivery or performance, both of you may be heading for trouble.

Not only is it stress and its impact that you have to deal with, as we have seen in the other related and specific chapters, but it will be your and your partner's communication skills within the intimate relationship of your marriage that will become a major issue to address. In such circumstances, begging for time and money to visit your parents abroad, may become an extremely difficult situation, especially in financially tight conditions.

It is not difficult to imagine how such problems would ripple wider and wider, and eventually soak through to the children. In the end, it is not only you, who are affected, but the whole family and its emotional qualities.

Parents back home

The same problem may arise for the family who stays behind, for example, your parents.

If you (as a parent) have had problems for years communicating your deeper feelings to your partner/spouse, or dealing effectively with your own losses, these feelings may unexpectedly recur in the present. However, they will do so gradually and be disguised by something else. Often, you only realize this only after your children have left the country for good.

You are not only confronted with the characteristics of your own life cycles related to ageing, and those of your marital life as it have developed in later years. You are also confronted with something new, like feeling you have lost your children, which may bring about a deep realization that the difficulties between you (as parents) should have been addressed many years ago.

Most of the time, the understanding of the impact that these problems have caused over the years is suddenly intensified by the shocking realization that your children may have left the country for good. This shock often becomes the trigger for things, which you have already experienced for a long time, and what seems so frightening, is actually your emotional response to this knowledge.

Luckily, you never become too old to change your mind, but you must look at those stumble blocks built up over years.

By having held desperately onto certain beliefs – in many cases outdated or non-applicable – you, the people back home, could have lost sight of what really matters. You need to acknowledge this to yourselves, and then pluck up the courage to tackle these set ideas.

One such belief may be taking the wedding vows literally by deciding that you would never sleep in different beds except when hospitalised, not even for a short while. Such set ideas can become problems in changed circumstances.

You greatly miss your children abroad, but would not consider buying only one plane ticket if you could not afford two. Nor might you want to accept the children's gift of tickets in the hope that the children would rather use the money to return, a remarkable thought with which you can empathize however, not always that realistic.

You forget to think about how deep the children's yearning can be to have you with them, at their overseas house, to see the grandchildren going to school, to be there for a birthday or two, in other words, experience how they are living their daily lives.

Of course, there are situations in which single trips would not be wise and this should be discussed with each other and the children, and accepted, if it is not possible to change things.

Sometimes solutions or options for different thinking are just around the corner. A retired professional or skilled parent may perhaps consider offering his or her expertise to similar positions overseas, and have the opportunity to visit the children at the same time.

There are several medical doctors and teachers who are retired in their own country but still act in locum positions abroad. Needless to say, it helps if they have been long-term clients of a specific recruitment agency, and hold citizenship of the country in mind.

'Were it not for these opportunities to stand in for colleagues at UK hospitals, my wife and I would not have had the chance to see our granddaughter growing up. We come at least once every 18 months, for a couple of weeks, and they try to visit us about every third year.' These were the thoughtful words of Ian, a general practitioner and dear friend, at the time based in Ireland. He sadly passed away since, and we now cherish his memory, having learnt from him and his family's positive attitude in dealing with the impact of emigration and living broad.

Ongoing relationships

How emotional issues are dealt with will impact on the quality of ongoing relationships. In the case of emigration, new roles are defined almost continuously, especially during the first phases of the process of transitional change. You could say that the first thing to go in a new country is those (often precious) known roles, and with them, certain traditions.

This can take a long time to establish itself as an identified area in the transitional process. It will also need to be addressed specifically on an ongoing basis. It is these transitions that hold the secret to successful adjustment and positive resettlement.

If you understand that you and your family members have to go through individual changes with their attached emotional features, you will understand that the issues of transition into the new immigrated life will be reflected in these ordinary cycles of change, in many different ways.

Developmental phases of a family

The nuclear family (father, mother and child/children) goes through its own cycle of development and change. This happens in addition to its members' individual emotional cycles, and their different phases of development and change.

It implies that several separate cycles are thrown together in the immigration melting pot, which will eventually have molded its individuality into newly shaped cycles and along with it, new behavioural patterns, according to each person's personality.

Psychologists and social workers will confirm what, for example, a couple with a new baby will tell you. Once the child is born the parents' relationship starts to change. They have to make new adjustments to their daily routine, their sex life, their relationship with their grandparents, work arrangements, and many more. Although they still love each other, they have to share each other with the child or children.

Previous expectations of the two of you as a couple in a loving relationship need to be reassessed and adjusted. Goals have to be reset and new roles need to be identified and respected.

This situation intensifies in the case of reconstituted families when a divorcee or widowed person joins a single parent family. Usually, these two families who are thrown together, each one with its own strengths and weaknesses, emotional baggage and subjective interpretations, will have additional issues to face and deal with. The new family develops as the children grow up and go through their individual stages, just as the parents do.

When you are living abroad and have the same family issues to address, whilst also trying to adjust to the challenges of emigration in general, you have to accept that these factors are likely to have an even bigger impact on all of you.

The good news is that once you realize this, you have set foot on the socio-psychological ladder towards working through these challenges, one by one, as they arise over time.

People tend to cling to known family patterns and roles that are out-dated in new settings. With immigrants this can become a desperate emotional exercise. The mother may be breadwinner in the new country, and no longer has the time and energy to fulfill her previous housewife-always-available-mother-at-home role, as before.

The father, who traditionally used to be head of the family and the household, may now have to take up the role of housekeeper, carer, child-minder, supportive spouse, babysitter, cook, and so on.

This is not hypothetical – it is a reality, especially in countries where child-minders and crèches are so expensive that the parent, who does not hold the work permit, has to stay at home to look after the children.

Taking on these roles with the consequences they hold, can be a painful experience for those who have difficulties adapting to change, and whose self-esteem comes from their initial role in the family unit.

It is especially difficult when the man had not expected this, and had planned on finding a job overseas so that his wife/partner could spend maximum time with the children, in order to assist in their adjustment to a new life.

For some working mothers, emigration brings intense feelings of guilt, more so than back at home. She now has to deal with her own feelings, as well as a home-husband who is often depressed about his circumstances, to whom she cannot look up to like before, and who increasingly leaves all the decision-making to her.

It is easy to blame it all on the emigration, when in fact there may already be serious underlying communication problems, causing negative and emotionally draining thoughts and feelings, which in the new circumstances can easily spiral out of control.

Often, couples who have previously managed their own bank accounts, now have to work with a joint account in the new country because only one partner has an income, or if the other partner still has one, it often is not nearly enough to justify a separate account. Issues of control may start to surface. Often, this result in serious marital conflict, and divorce may become the only option.

If you are prepared for the consequences that a change in financial circumstances may bring, you will be able to talk about the potential impact on your roles, needs, and financial expectations, before the time. Do it before you sell your home and leave your country and your security. If you have worrying doubts, and uncertainty that already disturbs your feelings of emotional security, consider postponing your emigration until these are sorted.

It is not negative thinking to imagine and consider worse case scenarios for what might happen when you are in the new country. These could be:

- If your partner does not find a job (which often happens)
- If you cannot afford childcare (which becomes reality for many)

- If your children cannot adjust (they do exist)
- If the partner with the work permit loses his or her job (as has happened in Britain during the recent recession)
- If you cannot adjust to the lifestyle of the new country (you know yourself)
- If you do not have the money to return home (which happens to many)
- If you have accumulated uncontrollable debt (which can easily occur once you are in an expensive country)
- If you cannot afford to retire in the new country

It does not mean that you will become stuck in negative 'what if' thinking. It means that you are realistically considering both ends of the spectrum, as there is often no return once you and your immediate family have started a new life abroad.

When discussing the power of negative thinking and realism, Chin-ning Chu[27] rightly says:

'It is not because of negativity that a cruise ship captain educates his passengers on how to behave in an emergency. He doesn't plan on having the ship sink. He is merely realistic and prepared.' (Chin-ning Chu, p.116)

I have met people who are such positive thinkers that they suppress all realistic patterns of thought, and bombard their partners with their unrealistic positivism. By rationalizing their desire to experience the excitement of new countries just because it has been a suppressed dream over years, these emotionally manipulative maneuver their partners into making the final decision to sell up and go (guess who will be blamed if things go wrong?).

Should the partner come up with 'what ifs,' these are usually tactfully wiped from the table as being of negative mindset. Sadly, I have met several immigrants in the United Kingdom who have had such experiences.

What saddens me more is that these partners so often stay in that relationship. They feel they have to because they hold the work permit, they are the parent who tries to hold the family together against the odds, or to divorce in an alien country without any support systems will be too difficult for them to handle.

Should you be in such a relationship, I would strongly advise that you seek professional guidance or counseling, as your strengths may be tapped beyond imagination once you are in the desired land.

However, with commitment to address your circumstances and to change your thinking from why to how, you will begin to develop a positive thought processing style. And you will discover your hidden inner strengths – but only if you really want to.

A family enters a new life cycle when the children get married and in-laws become new additions. For some, this does not always go as smoothly as desired, and it often depends on pre-existing expectations, sometimes realistic, but most often, unrealistic.

Sometimes parents want to choose their child's partner for different reasons. Similar cultural backgrounds appear to be one of the major perceived prerequisites to a successful marriage or long-term civil partnership.

When you live in a foreign country, it is likely that your child will fall in love with a local, as they will be forming peer groups, emotional attachments and bonding. (I recall somebody saying to me: 'Yes, we are still Afrikaans, but our children are English.')

Social psychologists, Robert Baron and Donn Byrne, refer to research studies carried out by several researchers on propinquity and friendship, and its effect on choosing a marriage partner.[28] The results of the different studies over the years showed that there was a tendency for people to end up with a partner or friend who lived in the same area as he or she used to live.

Although this does not mean that we will only be interested in people from our own area, it does reveal some tendencies towards such specific choices. Perhaps it is because of continuous exposure to the person, which leads to feelings of 'seeing that familiar face again.'

'The general idea is that we respond with at least mild discomfort to anything or anyone new. With repeated exposure we become desensitized, anxiety decreases, and that which was new becomes familiar.' (Baron & Byrne, p. 270)

There are also those who married partners who were fellow countrymen and women in the host country and decided to return to their original country as a couple. What a wonderful thought, you may think, but beware; there are serious pitfalls to watch out for. Sometimes sentiment about your country of origin, or intense homesickness, can make you vulnerable to choosing a relationship with somebody from your own country just because this similarity exists.

Parents may also be at fault. They should be on the lookout for their own misplaced yearnings and dreams in this regard, which they unconsciously (and often consciously) project onto the children. Often, they want their child to marry someone of the same origin, as an emotional deposit into their own dream-bank of returning home. They may think and hope that the newlyweds will return to the country of origin and that naturally, they will be obliged to go, too.

On the other hand, there are also parents who strongly encourage their child's engagement in relationships with local men or women purely because they do not want the child to return to the original country. They fear that the child will marry someone from their own country and return home, whilst the parents want to stay, or they think that it is not in the child's interest to return to his or her country of origin.

How challenging this can become! You will have to remind yourself regularly that it is your child's life, and he (or she) has the right and privilege to make his or her own choice in life (certain religions and cultures differ in this view). You should respect these wishes and choices. He will always value your support in letting him take responsibility for his own life.

This could be a good time to reconsider your preset values and beliefs about what you initially had in mind for your child. It could ask again for new adjustments within your overall adjustment to your immigration – and often at a time when you feel that you have finally made it, emotionally, in your new destination.

If you are the foreign addition to your lover's family, do respect their sentiments, cultural beliefs and customs. Do not forget that you have a different framework of reference and that their judgments are not necessarily wrong. They are simply different to yours.

You may even come to love and adore these differences in the end! They could become the funny things that you and your partner will lovingly joke about in the future (in private, of course!).

The next cycle in your own family life makes its appearance when the children leave the nest to start their own lives, get married, and start their own families. During these times, you also move into the next psychological developmental phase, for example, becoming a grandparent, and later, if you are so blessed, also a great-grandparent. These new cycles have their impact too - not only on your new identity, but also on the relationship between you and your spouse, and you and your children within the systems of the extended family.

Returning home – reversed emigration

If you had planned to return to your home country at retirement age, your children's living circumstances and their family lives in the adopted country might at this point, interrupt your plans significantly.

Once again, you will be confronted with the cycle of change and its subsequent adjustments, just like in the beginning when you and your children moved abroad and had to settle in a new country. This time, the emotional upheavals may be very difficult for the family to deal with, especially if the children want to stay, and you feel you must return.

For any ex-pat who wants to return to the country of origin, there are similar factors to consider and you have to think very clearly about such a change. You have to make a hundred percent sure if this is what you really want, and that it is not only an emotionally driven decision.

Again, there will be cycles within cycles, and you will have to face the consequences of your choices. It again will be a process consisting of stages, linked with intense emotions, realizations, times of disappointment and disillusionment, cultural adjustments, and also happy times.

There, again, will be a honeymoon phase and once it is gone, you can feel stuck, just like when you were in the process of adapting to your country abroad; and you will go through the process of loss again, this time yearning for what you have left behind somewhere in your country of acquired belonging.

To come home after a long period of time having lived abroad, is to put the process of emigration into reverse. This process can be just as stressful - you will have to deal with transitional change once again, and this time you will grieve over family and country life that have changed, with old surroundings suddenly be new and not that emotionally familiar to you like in the past, before your emigration to the country abroad.

Back home you will, again, find yourself swimming the ocean of your choice, driven by your inner drive to be and to stay home – sometimes against the currents, other times floating with their directions. And once again, you will find new strength to deal with your home coming; but, like before, only if you want to.

Despite all the ups and downs, disappointments and challenges, highs and lows, emigration can also hold a wonderful new life for many families. I have seen many happy emigrated families living abroad, and of those who have returned.

Like those back home, these families have certain features in their make-up and functioning, and you will recognize these when you meet them:

- They bond closely, but allow for differences and individual needs for emotional exploration in the new country
- They prioritize family life
- They communicate their feelings
- They listen to one another with an open mind and heart
- They celebrate their individual and family achievements
- They plan, play and pray together
- They forgive and move on
- They enjoy one another's differences
- Every day, they look for something to enjoy
- They focus on inner enrichment
- They allow themselves to grow spiritually
- They stick together but are flexible
- They acknowledge that what they have is strong enough to be able to let go when the time comes
- They continue to love

Exercise 4:

Perhaps there are more characteristics of your family that you want to add and to consider. Think about it, and write them down in the space below, replacing 'they' with 'us.' Add as many pages as you wish.

....

....

....

....

....

....

....

....

....

....

....

....

....

....

....

....

....

....

....

....

....

Discuss these with one another.

Part II:

Addressing the challenges

'Destiny is not a matter of chance, it is a matter of choice; it is not a thing to be waited for, it is a thing to be achieved.' (W.J. Bryon: Speech in Washington, February 22, 1899)

Chapter 8
Dealing with stress effectively

We previously said that stress can also be positive and that some people actually thrive on it. Who are they, and how do they deal with the same type of pressure that John and Sarah were exposed to?

They are the people who, as a starting point in their lives, practice self-honesty and acknowledge that transitional change is an ongoing entity that they assess and adapt to on an ongoing basis. They do not desperately wait for things to happen, but effectively plan ahead and face the challenges that they meet along the way.

They acknowledge the effects of stress, and they learn how to deal with it, addressing the way that they think about life's issues.

How you define stress for yourself depends on your own subjective experiences and your perceptions of these experiences, but especially in the meaning that you attribute to the trigger of your stress reaction. It is said that even this specific reaction to the stressor is a chosen one, and mostly, it happens unconsciously.

Should you wisely decide not to give stress free reign in your life, you would firstly, choose to first assess the real nature and cause of the stress and stressor to see if you can do something about it. This is a positive, constructive reaction.

In addition, there are several mechanisms, which you could build in, develop and streamline to suit you and more importantly, apply to your thinking and your actions in daily life.

Whether you make it in the new country depends on various factors. You must be motivated to actively develop your stress combating systems, and you must not get lost in bewildering thoughts, with undefined feelings directing your actions.

Additionally, you must be able to set and reset goals. Should you have problems in doing so, you need to recognize and acknowledge that you do have such a problem. Then you will be more able to do something constructively about it. This will help in managing stress, too. If your difficulties continue, look for professional guidance sooner rather than later, before stress prevents you from becoming the person that you want to be, and really are.

The skills that you will develop in your attempts to combat harmful stress, are usually transferable skills that can be used in several situations.

Aside from the more obvious things that you can do, there are the more deep-seated aspects of your personality, which you can use wisely to manage your stress levels in the new surroundings, for example, your emotional hardiness and congruency.

Psychological hardiness and resilience

Psychologists refer to a person's level of hardiness as being those aspects within his personality that equip him to address certain difficulties and to resist stress, as part of his emotional make-up.

The results of significant research on people's emotional hardiness have identified three components typical of a mindset, which indicates stress hardiness. These components are personal control, challenge and commitment.[29]

In contrast to the view that stress is an overwhelming force, which may paralyze you emotionally so that you lose all motivation and eventually become mentally and physically ill, they emphasize that stress can be motivational and challenging. If people learn how to understand their stress properly, they would be able to challenge it in positive ways.

The researchers indicate that emotionally hardy people resist becoming demoralized and try to find ways to address their difficulties so that they can gain and maintain personal control. For example, if they lose their job, they will reset their goals and try to find something compatible to their own values, so that they feel that they have some control over their own destiny.

Health psychologists[30] agree about the importance of personal control in maintaining stress hardiness. They have found that one of the significant culprits in stress is when a person experiences high demands from his environment whilst having low control over it. For example, if they are in a job where they take orders and have little, or no, say in things.

The research findings also identify that commitment to an active life of engaging in purposeful living becomes a significant component of the ability to resist stress. Even if there comes a time when you feel that almost everything is against you, you still strive towards resilience.

You view your life as having a purpose and you try to influence your surroundings for the better – and you persevere. You ask yourself difficult questions and you take risks in a mature and responsible manner:

'Resilient people find meaning in their activities even when faced with significant adversity precisely because they are committed to finding that meaning; towards taking an active, problem-solving approach to life.'
(Harry Mills, PhD and Mark Dombeck, PhD)[31]

Hardiness is something you can develop if you stay tuned to your inner self, your goals, work on your motivation, and persevere purposely. You need to stay optimistic in a realistic way, and work on your physical and mental health and fitness.

Congruency

The Latin word 'congruere' means to come together, to agree. In psychology and NLP we describe it as internal and external consistency, or the balance between self, others and context.

It is total alignment with your inner self, a state of being at peace with yourself, your goals, your values and everything that makes up your world. It is a state which others, when interacting with you, would describe as sincere and certain, and therefore most likely, emotionally solid, trustworthy and reliable.

Carl Rogers's well-known psychological Person-Centered Theory maintains that:

'Congruency is a high degree of similarity between what you experience in your immediate world and that which becomes part of yourself. If you would experience this, you would be congruent and emotionally healthy.'[32]

The way your personality functions and how you apply yourself would therefore mirror what is going on within you. From an inner state of congruency, you are resilient enough to influence your world from the inside out, instead of being influenced by the outside world, or from the outside in.

For example, were you an incongruent person, your attitudes, language, and way of presenting yourself would contradict your inner experiences. You may deny that you are jealous of others, because jealousy may be inconsistent with your image of yourself as a generous person. You become anxious and easily jump into defensive behaviour. You blame others for your failure, unhappiness and distress. You need to live a constricted life to guard yourself against any new experiences that may threaten a shaky self-image. In doing so, your personal growth is stifled.[33]

On the other hand, if you are a congruent person, you fight anxiety, phobias and defenses with resilience. This resilience is based in your unconditional self-worth, that so-called internal locus of valuation. You do not have to rely on defenses of distortion and denial, because there are no 'threats' from your outside world that you want to exclude from your awareness. You go for what are 'right' and 'true' and therefore, you are able to influence your surroundings positively. You 'go with the flow'.

During the initial phases of living abroad, especially in a country very different to yours, you will obtain information that will touch you cognitively and emotionally. You then have to draw heavily on your congruence and emotional hardiness. If you have problems in this regard, consider discussing this with a mental health professional or coaching psychologist.

Focused coping skills

There are two general ways of coping – by maintaining a strategy, which is either problem-focused (instrumentality), or emotion-focused (emotionality). [34]

The problem-focused person tries to reduce the demands of the stressors in his life, and increase available resources by which he can manage the stress more effectively. If you are a problem-focused person, you will do specific things to alleviate you and your family's stress in the new surroundings. You would draw up an 'agenda' of certain difficulties that you and your loved ones are experiencing. You plan how to address these, and you organize counseling sessions when you notice that relationships are starting to show signs of possible disintegration.

If you are somebody who practices emotion-focused coping strategies, you target the emotions involved. In doing so, you may like to use both cognitive and behaviour strategies to regulate these emotions.

These could be talking to someone about the problem, or even, as in less fortunate cases, resorting to negative behavior like excessive alcohol or drug consumption. This is something which appears to be a significant problem for immigrants and might result in offending behaviour. It can lead to a person ending up in the criminal justice system of the host country. Several probation officers and psychiatric staff in London have confirmed this phenomenon.

However, you could and should always resort to positive behaviour strategies. Continue to focus on your positive development. Learn new practical and emotional skills, not only to make yourself more employable, but to strengthen your self-esteem.

Language

It is not difficult to understand how quickly stress can snowball when you find yourself surrounded by everything 'alien', and when, in addition to culture shock, you are engulfed by the host country's language, so foreign to yours. You have realized by now that the immigration melting pot does not only harbour one common language. In London alone, there are over 300 different languages spoken every day.

One day, you may suddenly realize that you have almost forgotten to speak your own language; you even think in the new language, even if you sometimes still speak your own language at home, or with close friends who are also from your country.

To say that it is important to learn the new country's official language, is an understatement. If you can tackle this language and try to learn the idiomatic expressions too, you will feel empowered and your self-esteem will improve significantly.

Language is the link to all communication, and communication is the link to meaningful existence. That is what differentiates us from animals – the fact that we have words.

If you have real difficulty using the 'new' language, this may impact heavily on your ability to communicate and develop trustworthy confidants. And you need a confidant, be it a professional, an acquaintance, or a friend.

Confidants

It is said that many immigrants often feel misunderstood, undervalued and unworthy. Sometimes, due to the traumatic experiences of the process of loss and grief caused by their emigration, they tend not to trust or open up to others easily.

They may also feel that the locals will never understand them, as they 'have not gone through what we have gone through'. In certain respects they are quite right, but as an immigrant, you have to work on your abilities to develop trust again. Therefore, language barriers have to be mounted and overcome.

Talking

When you are uncertain about things in your new surroundings and you become aware that this is having an impact on your personality and functioning, talk to a trusted person, preferably a professional outsider. In this way, you will voice your own thoughts in a constructive manner and get a better picture of the reality of your situation. During this process you will become more objective, and able to judge your situation more realistically. You will begin to see things more clearly.

Talk to your partner and children. Acknowledge your partner, and be honest about your decisions and the reasons for making them. Listen to him or her, and express your understanding in an empathetic way. Partners often do not want solutions, but only a loving ear that listens and a heart that understands. In such a way they can talk on a deep, spiritual level.

Prioritize

When you are under stress, you may feel overwhelmed with thoughts and ideas, and find it difficult to come up with solutions. Now is the time to prioritize. Even if everything is important, there is always one thing more important or more urgent than the other. Be patient with this process.

The ability to prioritize can be a powerful tool in handling stress. To prioritize means you have to look at what is really important in your life. Which people are the most important to you? Which relationships are the most meaningful, and why? Can you answer this honestly? Can you write them down and read them out loud? If you cannot, why not? Is your first priority perhaps to address this honestly, before you move on?

Exercise 5:

Think about these questions and write down your answers. You can add to these as time passes.

Which people are the most important people in your life? ....

....

....

....

....

....

....

....

....

Which relationships mean the most to you?

....

....

....

....

....

....

....

....

....

Why?

....

....

....

....

....

....

....

....

....

If it is difficult to write these down, why?

....
....
....
....
....
....

Why is it easy to write them down?

....
....
....
....
....
....
....

Finances

Most of the time financial strain is part and parcel of the process of emigration. Develop skills in financial discipline, especially if you have had trouble with this in the past.

Learn how to budget, and be constantly aware of the dangers of accumulating debt.

Credit arrangements may differ from those in your home country. Before you sign up for any financial arrangement, scrupulously check the terms and conditions first.

If you know you can trust yourself with your finances, you can relax more easily. If you are more relaxed, you will be able to see things in a different, more positive light, and be able to find solutions.

Robert Kiyosaki is one of many financial experts, and writes extensively on financial matters and ways to address difficulties in these areas. [35] By reading as much as possible about finances, economy and labour law, you will guard yourself against unwelcome surprises. Become knowledgeable, and this will improve your self-esteem and emotional hardiness.

You may be surprised to learn that these skills, once learned and practiced, become transferable and can therefore be applied to different situations in life, work and play. They are not only characteristics, but specific ways of behaviour, and display a specific attitude, as well as qualities which can be practiced and developed into useful coping skills.

To cope with stress means to acknowledge that you are no different to other people, and that you may be susceptible to the impact of your new surroundings on different levels –spiritually, cognitively, socially and emotionally – because we all are emotional beings, so acknowledge that. If we had no emotions, life would have no meaning.

There may come a time when you have to acknowledge that your previous coping styles do not work so well any more. The new situation may call for something more creative, or simpler, than those problem-solving strategies that you employed in the past.

Marina did just that. She came to England to develop a career in social work, but when she realized that her expectations had not been met, she opted for teaching mathematics to troubled children. Having allowed herself to grieve her professional loss, she purposefully and optimistically worked towards her new goal.

Teaching mathematics to troubled children, whilst applying her psychological and social work skills unobtrusively, had provided an opportunity to develop both their IQ and their EQ (emotional intelligence). At the same time, she grew and developed much more than she would have done if she had stayed in her comfort zone.

Her success was based on refocusing, and being determined to reach her new goal. She realized that her basic needs in relation to work also had to be met, and so she chose a different, but related, profession in which she could develop her emotional and cognitive skills as well as those of the children, simultaneously.

She had moved her focus from troubled families in society, to troubled children in a specific setting. The method and outcome was slightly different but, in many ways, still the same, focusing on growth and development.

Isabel, 22 years old, described herself as a city girl and in many respects was thinking globally when she spoke enthusiastically about her experiences of life in London, prior to our interview.

We were sitting in a restaurant near Trafalgar Square and I saw her eyes sparkle with a deep sense of satisfaction, of knowing that she had made it. She had been lucky to find a job that she liked, and she had the emotional support of a loving family back home in Spain. Her determination was a mark of her character.

I asked her if things had always been in her favour. No, she said, this had not always been the case, for she had to return to London a second time, after a period lasting several months when she had struggled to find a job. She had problems with the expensive living conditions in London and had to deal with her feelings of sadness, disappointment and uncertainty on a daily basis.

This was a young Spanish woman born from a German father and Argentinean mother, who wanted to fight her way through life by herself, and her story resembles those of many young people who go abroad for the experience and psychological enrichment that it brings.

Isabel's parents supported her emotionally and when she decided to return to London, they allowed and encouraged her to do so, as they had realized that her personality would not allow her to leave things unfinished.

Again, she had to complete what she had started. Her second trip to London was again in good faith, but this time she had very clear goals in mind. She made use of social contacts, which she had developed over time, and soon found that she marveled in the vibrancy of the city, with its multicultural lifestyle and inhabitants from all over the world.

Unfortunately, not everybody can do that. Some of the people I spoke to revealed that they had acknowledged to themselves early on that they could not and did not want to make the necessary changes to their personality and lifestyle. They intrinsically knew that the best thing for them was to take stock and return home, to view the move to another country as a good experience from which they could learn. This was a sign of development in its own right.

Anetha, a professional Polish interpreter who left her family in Poland temporarily to develop her career opportunities and earn some money to start an independent life, joined me for coffee in the outskirts of London's East End. She was looking forward to reuniting with her family, who were expecting her back in Poland within the following days.

We talked openly and spontaneously about the ups and downs of foreign life, adapting to the new, and the experience of being alone in another country and on a self-assigned mission.

It was at this point that she pointed to her heart, as if wanting to hold and protect it from something unseen, and she said: 'One day I felt a funny but real and strong pain in my chest, and I recognized it as being in exactly the same spot as a pain I had experienced back in Iceland, which was my first foreign destination away from home.'

She described a feeling of deep sadness, a strange hurting, something physical – for unaccountable emotional loss at the time.

For her, the emotional pain of being an unwanted foreigner still lingered despite the fact that she was on her way back home after a couple of years abroad. She still hurt, but was psychologically richer and more mature.

'There have been very difficult times,' she said thoughtfully. 'The locals here do not accept you easily, just like in Iceland.' But what was apparent to me was her strong character, drive, ambition and determination to finish what she had started, so that she could look back and truly say: 'I have made it.'

She highlighted her determination and inner drive in achieving a pre-set goal as the one positive thing, which helped her getting through the tough times. One such plan was calculating beforehand the amount of money that she needed to earn in Iceland and London.

When at first she was unhappy because of the locals' often discriminating attitudes towards her, just like many other immigrants have experienced all over the world, she realized that by throwing herself into her work, she might survive.

The long months of Iceland's cold, wintry darkness did not help at all. It brought about low moods and significantly decreased energy, a condition that she had to confront and fight on a daily basis.

'Depression is all over. So many people suffer depression here because of the lengthy darkness,' she explained. But Anetha had clearly-defined goals, despite suffering from the condition, Seasonal Affective Disorder. She purposefully addressed her low moods to complete the full time period in Iceland, which she had pre-planned carefully.

Then London awaited her. A busy multi-cultural metropolis completely different to Iceland's wintry darkness and icy coldness, but with one claimed common factor: discrimination against foreigners.

She, like many others waitresses, was paid the minimum wage, not according to the legal requirements, which stated different minimum payment legislation according to age. When she challenged her employer, it was a matter of 'take it or leave it. I can easily get someone else to work for £4 an hour.'

This form of exploitation was also revealed by academic researchers at a symposium in London in June 2008, which introduced some research results regarding immigrants living in Britain.

Another barrier was no, or limited, recognition for academic achievements obtained in the home countries. Anetha, a Masters graduate in English, had to enroll again. When we met, she was busy with her final dissertations for a postgraduate diploma in translation. This however, was an example of her drive and ambition, which had pulled her through disappointments, challenges and ordinary, everyday life in another country.

It seems that a large number of those I had interviewed over time, have reached some kind of self-knowledge and emotional maturity through their hard and heartfelt years in a country away from their own. This stage of self-knowledge, is a, if not the most, crucial factor in successful overseas living and adjustment to the new.

Remember, however, that people differ and what is right for one is not necessarily right for the other. Stay true to yourself, acknowledge your strengths and move on.

Chapter 9
Dealing with change requires different forms of intelligence

We are not born with set wisdom and knowledge, and life's roads are not always highways and racetracks. Neither do our life journeys run smoothly. We are always being confronted with crossings, stop signs, traffic lights and roundabouts (traffic circles). Sometimes, in the most unexpected places, we have to make new decisions and choices about how and where to drive safely in order to reach our destination.

The wisdom and knowledge to deal with these choices and their consequences in a constructive and positive manner, is like driving a car, a skill that can be acquired. Some people have a natural flair for adapting to new problem-solving strategies and techniques, but many have to learn and to develop these skills purposefully and with a highly focused mind.

Therefore, the ability to solve problems or to change your circumstances, and to deal with the accompanying emotions and feelings in a constructive way, does not just happen automatically. It needs thorough assessment and thoughtful, clear decision-making both on a cognitive and emotional level.

The process of emigration and resettlement in a foreign country requires not only strong will, motivation and dedication, but applied intelligence in order to succeed, so that you can say: 'I have made it!'

The sort of intelligence needed does not refer only to your IQ (Intelligence Quotient), but also to other forms of intelligence that, when applied, will assist you in dealing with the process of transitional change. These are emotional, social and spiritual intelligence.

Integrated intelligence

Within the context of this book, integrated intelligence refers to a certain level of 'mature' development; something of wholeness. It is the integration of knowledge, feelings, emotions, cognitions – shortly everything external that needs to be internalized, or processed within the mind, in order to react pro-socially and emotionally healthy. It is beyond fragmented views and beliefs.

Therefore we can differentiate between the important aspects of intelligence, of which emotional intelligence, social intelligence and spiritual intelligence are some. Although we differentiate between these, they all form part of the developed person's personality make up, and his and her way of self-presentation and personal functioning.

By looking more closely to the different forms of intelligence, we shall see how they play significant roles in successful living.

Emotional intelligence

Considering the previous chapter, it is evident that emotional intelligence plays an important part in successful adjustment to new circumstances. But what exactly is emotional intelligence?

It is the type of intelligence which in effect makes up your emotional identity – what you are or what you have become. It refers to the knowledge, management and presentation of yourself, but especially to your level of emotional awareness. Your emotional intelligence has certain ingredients: those you have collected, sifted, and internalized over years of life experience. You have learned how to recognize when you should apply them, and which of them you need to apply.

It is not a given that everybody has been blessed with appropriate amounts of emotional intelligence. It is something which develops over time, through experience in different life situations, and by dealing with life's demands and people, starting from childhood.

It speaks of the fine balance between feelings, emotion and cognition where one need complements another so that you can reach your full capacity to be an asset to others, and to experience the meaning of consciousness.

It requires a sincere, honest look at your inner being. It demands that you acknowledge exactly what you see inside yourself, and to address this inner 'thing', or revelation, even if you do not like what you see. For this there are different approaches, as people are individuals and will move through the process of transitional change at different tempos. This will largely depend on their personalities and individual circumstances.

Having learned about John and Sarah on the one hand and Marina and Isabel on the other, we recognize the different approaches to coping and being, the detrimental outcome of unbalanced views, desperate and catastrophic thinking, and misplaced emotional spring tides.

Eventually, the core of the matter will be two simple, related concepts – self-honesty and self-knowledge. These can, however, be the most difficult things to apply to you. To be honest with yourself is to penetrate your own mind without armoury and shields, to look at your deepest feelings and to put these into descriptive words for yourself to understand, analyse and act upon.

In his book, *The Feeling of What Happens*, the psychiatrist Antonio Damasio describes feelings as something directed inwardly – an occurrence which happens inside a person, which others do not know about. This, he explains, gives rise to emotions which are projected outwards – the emotions which others can observe when they look at you and listen to you. Both feelings and emotions are, however, necessary to create consciousness and knowing. [36]

You can have feelings without being consciously aware of them. This usually happens in circumstances where you suppress them to maintain a low level of emotional awareness, and to protect yourself against the revelation of unresolved issues, that may be screaming for solutions.

This process has been happening in several immigrants' lives, especially those who have struggled to adjust to the new and to resettle successfully in a new country.

It may be that there are people who ran away from issues too difficult to deal with, without knowing exactly what they were running towards, or away from. My friend Antoinette, wisely said, when I told her about our plans to come to England: 'As long as you are running towards something and not running away from something.' I was running towards something.

Tom came to England for better work prospects two years ago, hoping he would find the pot of gold all his friends were talking about. He did not find the pot, or the rainbow, but he found a job providing reasonable pay and lots of opportunities to travel all over Europe, which he is still enjoying.

Yet, after many trips in other countries, he phoned to tell me about his joyful experiences, but in the same breath he voiced his inner turmoil: 'Why do I still feel unfulfilled and unsettled and craving home? Perhaps I should get another job – one that is more fulfilling. By the way, where exactly is home?'

Listening to him from across the small table of a street cafe in London's Soho, I could see his emotions reflecting deeper feelings about a difficult childhood that he still needs to come to terms with. He was emotionally rejected by his father, and had a demanding, neurotic mother, who was forever pushing him to excel academically by maintaining straight A's throughout high school. She did not provide the emotional warmth a developing child needs and this has impacted significantly on the challenging process of trying to find his own identity.

In England, he perhaps would find it by doing his own thing, by himself, for himself whilst still maintaining and satisfying some part of his philanthropic instinct. In this case, driven by sacrificing love and concern, wanting to repair things, by assisting his mother and siblings financially after his parents' divorce at the same time as he started planning a move to England.

'There are many Toms in life, not only those who have moved abroad,' I hear you say.

You are quite right, there are. The issue, however, is that the impact of having gone through emotional trauma without having worked through it, seldom becomes so real and scary, as when you are all alone far away from those you love and who love you.

But in the end, it is how you choose to deal with these underlying unresolved feelings and issues that will predict the outcome of your personal process of transitional change and eventually, the feeling of belonging in a new country.

Tom had to stop shielding himself against the painful experiences of his past. He started doing this by examining them one by one, putting them into words, and acknowledging to himself that these things had really happened. He allowed himself to feel the emotional pain that they had created and realized that very often he would still have the same feelings, but this time, they would be attached to something unknown to him, as if he was projecting them on to someone else.

One day, out of the blue, he realized that he was actually carrying this bag of feelings around with him, putting it anxiously onto his lap whenever he felt low, unpacking them and cuddling them until he felt drained enough to be able to say that others really had messed up his life, and that nothing would ever work for him – that coming to England was a mistake, and that it only intensified his loneliness.

He actually said to himself, aloud, that he had started enjoying his emotional baggage because it gave him some sort of identity – silly, he remarked, but true. He had been too reluctant to let go of it, as it would have left him alone in the cold. At least he now knew who he was, the rejected child born from his parent's stormy marriage.

By acknowledging this, he could then identify that unfortunately, he was actually turning his emotional baggage into a ball and chain, tying it to his leg to drag it with him through his life, thereby allowing the past to hold him back.

It is like having a part of yourself that has served you purposefully up to a point in your life. No matter how little good it brought about, it still served a purpose. For Tom, harbouring his past brought him a feeling of identity, even if it was limiting and twisting.

He now feels ready to embrace change.

Do these cases of Tom, John and Sarah reflect something about ourselves and our defenses, which we hoped would shield us against hurt and change? Just in case we get hurt again?

Whether you try to avoid pain and scars, or choose to grab the new energy emerging from the transitional process, you have to understand exactly what it means you are going through. Many psychologists agree that change cannot happen until repression has been lifted. Only then can the person let go of his or her defenses.[37]

As a prerequisite, you have to 'live' this process of transitional change by looking at its components, not only theoretically but from an emotional perspective. And to deal with it successfully you need to be emotionally intelligent.

If you do not understand this, you may experience the changes around you as being (very) difficult to address, unless you are an emotionless being who wants to avoid understanding what it means to live – or perhaps you have been hurt extensively and want to withdraw from feeling. It is, however, by living that we learn how to survive and how to become emotionally intelligent.

To me, it often appears as if the concept of 'emotionality' is too often crucified, because in many circumstances, it is defined by people with a limited framework of reference.

These people, sometimes ignorant and other times just not aware enough, tend to classify or run down the meaning of emotionality according to their own limited framework of reference – sometimes for reasons unknown to themselves, or perhaps known, but too hard to face.

The example of Sarah in a previous chapter reminds us of a person keeping her emotional turmoil alive, and this had become a means in itself. It created her identity, because she had chosen her feelings to shape that identity.

Therefore it is not at all strange that her identity had eventually subsided. Her reluctance to learn new coping skills to address her high levels of stress, actively and purposefully, had contributed to the process of shaping an identity, which may raise serious concerns.

You need to know and understand that although you feel sure about your identity now, relocating to another country will eventually, in most cases, mean finding a new identity. This will consist of the known, unknown and the unexpected – born from the challenging process of transitional change. How you are dealing with your emotionality will dictate, in many ways, your success in moving through the different processes of identity formation.

So, how do you really understand emotionality? What does it mean to you?

Exercise 6:

Define the word 'emotionality' by free-thinking: write down as many words and phrases as possible that you associate with the word 'emotion.'

(i) Sit down and relax, and when the words pop in your mind, write them down as quickly as possible without thinking too hard.

....
....
....
....
....
....
....
....
....
....
....
....
....
....
....

(ii) Underline all the verbs – words indicating action, occurrence or being.

(iii) Using a different colour, underline all the adjectives – words indicating a description.

(iv) Now, look at these thoroughly, think about what you see emerging, and write down your own definition of the word 'emotionality.'

....
....
....
....

....
....
....
....
....
....
....
....

(v) Did your definition change? ....
....
....
....

(vi) Write down how you think this changed definition may affect your feelings and behaviour in future.

....
....
....
....
....
....
....
....
....
....
....
....

Emotionality – a deeper look

Looking at your answers to this exercise, you would already know that you are delving much deeper than just the general 'knowing' of superficial self-screening, or just answering for the sake of answering.

You are looking deeper, wanting to look deeper. Let us then analyse the word 'emotionality' together, and for the purpose of this exercise, in the following way:

e-mo-tion-a-lit-y

e- (Latin) this reminds of electronics i.e. e-mail, in other words something programmed onto something

-motion- movement, moving from one place to the other

-a- : very specific

-lit- : linked to light (verb and noun)

The words motivation and emotion originate from the Latin word 'movere'. An emotion is something very specific; it moves you from one point in your psyche to the next. If you look at how it works in your neuro-psychological make-up and how it is transferred from your inside to the outside world in the form of noticeable features, like a happy smile, the emotion will light you up. The result? You may feel very good, even wonderful, for having let it out. Can you remember that time when you roared with joyful laughter? Do you remember how you felt afterwards?

In the case of anger, which can be noticed in the tension around the eyes and mouth, you will feel bad, or even worse than bad, if you let the anger out in unacceptable ways.

Emotions and feelings are not the same, although they are both associated with the emotional brain, the limbic circuit, as explained in the previous chapter on stress.

We know now that feelings are on a personal, inner level and that they are directed inwards, while emotions are projected outwards and therefore observable to the outside world.

The intensity and way in which you are going to project your feelings to the outside world will depend on the meaning that you add to the content, and are based on your previous experiences and subjective interpretations of these. These interpretations reflect your values and norms.[38]

You could say that your emotions motivate you, or move you, but that they also dis-empower you if you would allow them to override reason, like in the case of anger when it would manifest itself in aggressive and destructive actions.

Emotions are with us whenever and wherever. The issue, however, is if and how we are going to allow them to direct us, especially during the process of transitional change when behaviour resulting from stress can become imminent and emotions extremely powerful. The crucial factor will be what we are going to do with the emotions once we have become aware of them.

As a first step, you need to define the emotion, word it out loud and verbalize it. Saying it out loud acts as a confirmation of your thoughts, because you hear it and therefore realize and acknowledge to yourself that it exists. It is especially helpful to do this when you are in conflict, doubt, confusion or if you feel overwhelmed and hurt.

It is very often during the earlier phases of the process of re-settling in a new country (or any other unfamiliar place far away from the old one) that this happens. During these times, usually after the honeymoon phase is over, you become more aware of the major losses that you and your loved ones have suffered due to your emigration - and the fact that you have given up so much to make it work in the new country.

You may find that your relationships do not prosper or that you feel emotionally drained and continuously tired, and even a little bit fed-up. However, if you look around you, you see something completely in contrast to how you feel. You know you have to acknowledge that you have everything you have planned for in the new country: a home, a job and new friends indicating that they welcome you despite the fact that you are a foreigner. Even your family looks happier.

But in the meantime, you feel as if you just cannot move on, as if something heavy pulls you back and prevents you from moving on, keeping you from becoming the resourceful, resilient and robust person you had been before your emigration.

A previous chapter on change identified this as part of the first stage of the process of change and re-settlement in the new surroundings. But it stretches deeper as it asks something from you emotionally, namely to identify these feelings, and link them to certain emotions which you project to the outside world. This is not necessarily easy, because you have to admit to yourself that you do have these feelings and emotions, and that you exhibit these actions or behaviour.

These could be slightly observable actions of discontent, irritation, frustration or keeping your distance, which your colleagues or manager may observe at work - or your family members who feel slightly at a loss with your mood swings, as if you are somebody they do not really know any more.

When looking into yourself honestly, and thereby practice unguarded, truthful introspection, you may find that the feeling which actually may be causing these emotions (and therefore actions), is mostly your reaction to the loss of security that you have suffered due to your emigration.

You will see that underlying your emotions are the unresolved feelings of anger – the feeling that you have lost something and someone meaningful to you. Like Bridges would have said: 'a feeling that something or someone has done you in.'[39] (Consider reading again the chapter on loss before moving on.)

Mingled with this loss occurring on different levels, is also the impact of having been exposed to overwhelming new circumstances, also on different levels; challenges that you have to meet right from that first moment in the host country.

Social Intelligence

There may be different opinions on what social intelligence is exactly. Different professions like Anthropology, Biology, Psychology, Sociology and Neurology (to name just a few) would define it from their respective viewpoints, linking it to their theoretical frameworks and providing us with fascinating research results. Within the emigrational context many of these would apply, but it is the findings in the field of socio-neuro-psychology that are perhaps the more alarming ones. As immigrants, we can name or refer to several significant social encounters which would mirror many such findings.

Referring to the role and significance of neural dynamics in human relationships, Daniel Goleman describes the social brain as the sum of the neural mechanisms that orchestrate our interactions, thoughts and feelings about people and our relationships. Other than our biological systems that regulate their activity in response to signals from within the body, the social brain functions uniquely in its sensitivity to the world at large.[40]

'Whenever we connect face to face (or voice to voice, or skin to skin) with someone else, our social brains interlock.' (Goleman, 2006, p. 11)

How we connect with others would therefore be significant in our key relationships, as these can gradually mould certain neural circuitry, and would thereby bring about changes in our social neurological pathways. How and if it happens would very much rely on the level of rapport created between the people who need to connect.

During the first phases of your process of transitional change in a new country, it may be that you seldom experience rapport with those around you, as there may still be too little about the others which you can identify with. You have to build up meaningful connections and relationships before you can truly experience rapport.

This special connection, rapport, is more than merely social ease and a comfortable feeling when being with someone else. It entails shared positive feelings, mutual attention and mutual interests that would create some bonding with the other. It has a special element of trust and creates emotional warmth, a state of empathy you can rely on. Its level of communication indicates caring and congruency.

Often the first elements of real connections happen in the workplace, as this becomes the place where you spend most of your time with many others, mostly from different backgrounds, but with one common goal – the shared mission of the organization or company. Connections also occur at regular religious gatherings where you can join with like-minded spiritual companions.

You should keep in mind that your children may make connections at their schools or with friends, you with your colleagues, but your spouse or partner, the homemaker, may miss out and start feeling excluded and lonely. Be socially and emotionally aware of this and act upon it. Regular social settings for you and your family, filled with the promise of rapport, would not only serve the interest of every one of you, but it would also help to cement the bonding between you all.

Good rapport implies a good feeling that stems from positive vibes between people, those non-verbal messages that form the large basis of the iceberg of communication. These are hidden in posture, facial expression, tone of voice, eye and hand movements: the pace and timing of conversation, whether verbally or non-verbally.

Being confronted with different cultures with their different ways of communication, especially different meanings that are added to similar gestures and words, may create more than just a feeling of uneasiness. It may develop conflict, distance, and the sense of a cautious attitude, also often feelings of distrust – all enough to put you on guard, thus avoiding building rapport.

If your travel bag has been filled with emotional and social intelligence, you would know that these sorts of initial feelings are only natural under the circumstances; they're real and expected. However, you would also know that you should apply your inner strengths and social knowledge and start reaching out to 'the other'. Even if you are the 'guest' in the country and the host, the country, would not feel that accommodating!

With honesty and congruency as part of your inner being, you will soon lay the cornerstone for healthy communication, rapport and coordinated connection. You will listen with full receptivity and understand the other on a deeper emotional level that shows accurate empathy and attunement to the other's feelings and intentions. These ingredients of social awareness are only the basis from where social facilitation flows. [41]

You facilitate socially when you synchronize or interact smoothly with another whilst presenting yourself effectively and empathically; when you influence and shape the outcome of your social interactions; and when your words and deeds show concern for the other.

It is said that it pays to add new people to your social network, especially trustworthy ones, to counteract anxiety and psychological 'angst'. Therefore, remember to reduce the number of emotional toxic interactions that will for sure come your way in your new world.

Rather increase the nourishing ones:

'Socially integrated people – those who belong to...social and religious groups, and participate widely in these networks - recover more quickly from disease and live longer. Roughly eighteen studies show a strong connection between social connectivity and mortality.' (Sheldon Cohen in Goleman 2007, p. 247)

Spiritual intelligence

This is nothing sinister, but rather, something very real – as real as the real person deep within you. It is you.

It is when you allow yourself the journey of developing your spiritual intelligence that you develop this inner part of yourself, this unarticulated part, or level of being which you cannot see or touch, yet, eventually do see something of it, and you eventually do feel its touch all over your existence.

If you allow it to be, or rather, allow yourself to be as it was meant to be right in the beginning, spirituality becomes your world. And this is a real world, not a head-in-the-clouds sort of thing, and definitely not madness.

Spiritual intelligence does not mean to be emotional, or being removed from reality and the real world. It also is not the world of spirits like in spiritism. Spirituality can be seen as a function from the universe, the reality of something greater than you of which you are part, but which is also part of you. It is the life that was blown into you, that distinguishes you from the rigidity and limitations of things.

The Royal College of Psychiatrists states that in healthcare, spirituality is identified with experiencing a deep-seated sense of meaning and purpose in life, together with a sense of belonging. They accentuate that it is about acceptance, integration and wholeness. [42]

They quote authors who define the spiritual dimension as that which is trying to be in harmony with the universe, striving for answers about the infinite and comes especially into focus in times of emotional stress, physical and mental illness, loss, bereavement and death.[43] Some authors talk about spiritualism in association with spirituality. Spirituality is not spiritualism.

"Spiritualism and the occult may share some elements, but they are not... the same. Spiritualism involves only the body's own spirit and the spirit of those things that surround it, that same spirit that separates us from the rocks and the dirt. Spirituality is defined solely by itself and its own identity, which distinguishes it from the practices of the occult." [44]

As you learn the power of sensitivity that comes with spirituality, it gives you wings and lifts you to more than just fulfilling your potential. It opens you up to a deep level of knowing, which will guide you, make you alert, and teach you in what is true.

You are created as a spiritual being – mind, body and soul - different concepts, yet, interwoven to one-ness; distinguishable, yet inseparable.

When you are confronted with life in an alien country, you may sometimes feel confused, overwhelmed and even exhausted as if to your sole. This alien country has become your new world, and when strange and different cultures accentuate in their being your own culture as being different, strange and even alien to others, you could feel marginalizedly alone, and this within 'your' new world.

In such circumstances, like in any other demanding situation of change or discomfort, you may tend to construct emotional and social defenses in an attempt to protect yourself from being invaded by the new. You forget to stay sensitive to others because your own emotional needs may have become upfront in your mind, and you could feel emptiness within.

Yet, should you be able to stay sensitive to the vibes from your environment, the people's inner messages transcended by their choice of characterizing who they are – dress, cuisine, religion, relaxation, education, actions – would be less of an emotional or social threat.

You need to be conscious of being tuned with your inner self, and the richness of its peace and knowledge when you allow your sensitivity to become spiritually attuned with your surroundings, would become a whole and wholesome experience. You have to allow for this sensitivity and spirituality to develop and become the real you, wherever you are - alone, in a group with others, or in a crowd.

And you will learn the secret of living – even within the demands and challenges of your emigration turmoil where change may continue to drift and to rule.

For, as change will be rippling wider and wider, and its global pond shrinks as minds and hearts continue to scream in their so often, senseless search for same, you will stand strong in the knowing that you are you.

Chapter 10
Culture shock

Culture shock is not only the shock of first impressions when you are confronted with an alien place and its alien people. Neither is it only that sudden feeling of aloneness when you are surrounded by a variety of cultures, on a bus or train, when you drive through London, New York, Delhi, Perth, or wherever your pre-planned destination had taken you. It is much more than that.

Why is it so overwhelming?

It may be completely overwhelming to experience that initial emotional exposure to the different surroundings of another country. No matter where you are from, you can easily feel overwhelmed in and by the new world. The intensity or degree of this emotion will depend largely on your personality, your level of acknowledged awareness, and how much previous experience of traveling abroad you have already had.

It is like coming from Africa into a European country, where you have to travel from the airport by underground rail ('Tubes' in London) when the only trains you have experienced before, have been single railway lines carrying you through a vast, peaceful African landscape. Or city lines where the only 'underground' is the platforms under the roof, like those at Johannesburg railway station.

You have learned English at school as a second language of equal status to your mother tongue, but then you arrive in England and find that you are not understood! Not only is your accent strange, but so are those of many of those of British people, too, who sometimes find it difficult to understand a fellow countryman. Not to mention the many different expressions for the same thing. I am sure this is not restricted to one country!

Have you ever felt that intense embarrassment when you are having an educated conversation with intelligent people, and you use the wrong (and I mean *wrong*!!) term when you are trying to say something? Like the Australian talking of thongs, or a South African or Italian looking for pants instead of trousers. Or an American woman searching for pantyhose on her visit to England, definitely not knitted tights, but only finding tights, which fortunately are the same as pantyhose back home!

If you visit London's East End, you will still be able to find real Cockneys who talk in rhyme in that strange, charming nasal tone of voice. 'You lookin' for the stairs? No luv, you will only fin' the "apples and pears".')

One day, I remember entering an office in North East London, where I used to work. Suddenly it was as if I were walking into an unknown country with its very strange, and to me, senseless, language: English, but also not English. All five staff members were talking Cockney. I could not believe that these were the same people I had been introduced to. Well, luckily they switched to 'London English' when they noticed me!

Then there are things like written public signboards and seldom the luxury of displayed signs or symbols. Beware the person who has difficulties reading and writing, and surprisingly, this is quite a significant percentage of residents in the United Kingdom. (Luckily both these issues are being addressed – the written directions at public places possibly in light of the fast approaching Olympic Games!)

On a more serious note, enjoying cultural diversity and its amazing vibrancy is one thing, but experiencing culture shock is something completely different. And it is only over a period of time that its intensity strikes.

That shock

Nowadays, a cosmopolitan city hosts and houses people from all over the world; people with different cultural backgrounds that are reflected in their looks, actions, dress, language, manner, religion, values and norms. In fact, in everything visible and invisible.

Phillippe Legrain's research indicates that migration between different countries is happening all the time, increasingly so. This implies that people are being confronted with cultural diversity all the time, which, eventually, is having an effect on their own identity issues.[45]

If you want to have a meaningful life in another country, then this is the time when you will need all aspects of your intelligence to address the issues arising from culture shock. Being amongst totally different people, physically and psychologically, you may find initially that you tend to cling to your own culture to sustain your known identity.

For some, it is interesting and challenging to engage daily with people from all over the world, especially if they are strange in their difference. It may press that inner button, revealing an unconscious desire to be different yourself, to combat tradition and your known cultural background, and to merge with those around you.

Sooner or later the time will come when you experience difficulties, like so many others: alienation, distance, and being marginalised – socially, emotionally and culturally –especially if you have difficulty in adjusting to your new surroundings.

Should this difficulty continue to be an issue, you may at some stage experience those electrifying feelings of alienation that make you feel even more distanced – almost detached and 'unreal'.

This reaction to your circumstances does not necessarily indicate a psychotic state, but if it interferes with your normal daily functioning, it will worry others, so if it continues, do consider professional counselling as a matter of urgency. It does not mean you are going mad, but it may be that you are experiencing an adjustment disorder, which is treatable and not at all uncommon.[46]

You can deal with the impact of culture shock effectively. Many people do. To do this, you will need different forms of intelligence, not just on a philosophical basis, but also in a practical way in your day-to-day existence in the new country.

Now is the time to unpack that luggage, the suitcase carrying your social, emotional and spiritual intelligence. By applying these strengths, your cultural experiences will eventually become a major part in your continued personal growth and enrichment.

It is necessary, however, that you at first recognize, understand and accept that culture shock does have an impact on you. That the problem is not the people around you or the unfamiliar and often strange surroundings, but it is actually the consequences of the thought-feeling-behaviour link within you – your thoughts and your reactions to what is going on around you, and how it impacts on you emotionally.

When culture shock knocks at your door, you can easily attribute the stress caused within you, to those around you. You may blame everything on 'these strangers', or on their cultural behaviour when they are from another orientation. Are you not just as foreign to them as they are to you?

Symptoms and reactions

Looking at the most common symptoms of culture shock and those of stress, loss and the different processes within the cycle of change, the similarities are amazing. Post Traumatic Disorder can be noticed on several occasions, however, not necessarily all of them.

The United Kingdom Home Office identifies the symptoms of culture shock as being:

- Extreme homesickness
- Feelings of helplessness and dependency, disorientation and isolation
- Feelings of depression and sadness, hyper-irritability, inappropriate anger and hostility

- Sleep and eating disturbances (too little or too much)
- Excessive critical reactions to the host country's culture, stereotyping and hypochondria.

There are excessive feelings of paranoia – fears and thoughts of being done in, taken advantage of and with that, distrust in what the new country may have to offer. It is also not unusual for people to have excessive fears of lack of sanitation and of consequential illnesses.

Recreational drug use and developing drug dependency as well as excessive alcohol use are common. It is not only due to the fact that immigrants may be more exposed to the faster flow of alcohol in a country like Britain, but that certain individuals misuse alcohol or drugs as an escape from having to address the more difficult consequences of their immigration.

They are already emotionally exhausted, an exhaustion that impacts destructively on their coping mechanisms when they are faced with extremely high demands. How much more when there are additional things they have to deal with in the new world of work, family and social surroundings, and all of these simultaneously.

Research into the effect of culture shock highlights the so-called U-curve that symbolises the process of one's emotional and social journey through these cultural effects.[47] It appears that it is only when you have travelled through this neuro-socio-psychological journey that you will be able to settle down.

Settling down in this sense does not only mean accepting your new situation and the differences to your own background, but rather settling down with new experiences of emotional flow and happiness.

Looking at the initial phase of culture shock, the excitement that characterises this honeymoon phase may quickly turn into a spontaneous tendency to highlight the differences in cultural characteristics, instead of the initial tendency to look for common factors between the two.

I remember my reaction during the initial phase of my adjustment to England. It came almost spontaneously. I would rather see those things which reminded me of home, and even looked for features in people or situations with which I could identify and associate with dear ones and places back home – something familiar and known in the unknown.

Culture differences which perhaps could be too much of a challenge at the time, were interesting, exciting to see and hear, but something that I, at that stage, would rather keep at arm's length. I still valued my own culture too much and thought of myself in the same way as I did before I left South Africa. I was not the immigrant. I was me, a South African living and working in London, respecting my host country and its people, but not part and parcel of it all.

Although I realized that I would have to integrate totally and in many ways become 'British' to be accepted by the locals as an equal, I still harboured my difference, as it gave me my own identity. This feeling lasted for months, if not years.

However, for many people this honeymoon phase can rapidly turn into a downward spiral heading to the bottom of the U-curve. They may experience intense difficulties in objectively assessing the cultures of the new country and also their own feelings and behaviour.

The tendency to escape through blaming and shaming behaviour by viewing cultural differences as defects and obstructions, as well as threats to society as a whole, may cause the person to become more alienated and, of course, increasingly lonely.

In this sense, expatriates can easily fall prey to the foreigner syndrome: clinging to your fellow countrymen, avoiding mixing with the locals, forming cliques with those from the same area as you (cliques within cliques), criticising locals, pushing yourself to form new communities of the same, and making locals feel unwelcome.

But you have to distinguish between these 'communities' – those which stem from a hard-wired mentality, and those which, over the ages, have naturally developed all over the world as immigration has increased.

People who naively believe that everyone sees the world from their eyes and departs from their framework of reference, are more likely to experience culture shock as disillusionment – an engulfing process of deepening emotional disaster that will drag them into the deepest depth of that U-curve.

This relates directly to subjective perceptions, often the result of emotionally loaded and confusing encounters. However, there is hope, as this phase does not necessarily last long – for some it is weeks and for others, months. The positive side to it lies in the opportunity that it gives you to do some thorough, and in-depth, self-assessment.

By looking at your issues in depth and dealing with them, you will be able to create your place in your new society. You will eventually discover your 'new' identity of person-in-a-bigger-world, of having become something of a globalised being. You will discover a new self-confidence, self-reliance and emotional independency. The enlightenment that comes with the realisation of the capability to deal with cross-cultural experiences effectively brings with it a feeling of pride and achievement.

I heard something about this in the words of my young British friend, David Morris, who loves travelling the world, all on his own. He told me about his different experiences in Peru, Japan and Australia, which mainly had to do with his perception and interpretation of those around him at the time.

For example, the complete difference of Japanese customs, which David experienced as being distanced and aloof, made him feel at times, extremely alone, threatened and alienated. Was the fact that he had to sleep overnight in a room the size of a coffin at a Japanese train station, representational of his perceived alienation in a country completely different to his own? Did it represent suppressed feelings of emotional death – a fear of the death of everything that is known and dear to you?

In Australia, David met up with other Britons in a pub (quite by chance!) and eventually ended up in a guest house where he was so overwhelmed with the hospitality of his hosts that he almost felt like family.

Having gone through a couple of years of happiness in a country so different to his own, he eventually enjoyed the ultimate sense of achievement the moment he arrived home, where his family awaited him. A deepened sense of emotional maturity engulfed him, all due to the experience of having gone through the process of change towards greater emotional independence and a higher sense of self-achievement.

The fact that David knew he could return home when he felt like it, and therefore had carefully budgeted for such an occasion, might have contributed to maintaining the positive and exciting side of culture shock – that of the initial honeymoon phase.

He knew there would be an end to it, and that he would return to England to a loving, longing family. He could also bargain on the support of trustworthy, caring Australians who became his friends during times when he had been desperately homesick.

He concluded his story by saying that a little culture shock certainly helps to immunise you against the shocks, which will reappear with future travelling.

'And what happens then?' I asked him. Then, once again, you dig into your bag of experience, he said. A bag filled with emotional, social and spiritual intelligence, and you take the bull by the horns.

On the other hand, for those who are living permanently, or for a next couple of years, in the new country of pre-planned destination, dealing with culture shock may be ongoing, something that continuously and consistently has to be addressed on a daily basis.

This will continue until you reach your eventual spiritual destination, the stage when you realize that you have to let things be – reaching a form of completion in an incomplete world of diversity. To understand diversity is, actually, to understand that diversity is not diversity, but that there is a oneness in the bigger whole of a so-called alienated world.

Culture shock is much more than the feeling of being trapped on an overloaded train on the Underground when the fragrance of today's perfume mixes with last night's garlic. Much more than seeing last year's broken dreams carved on tired city faces senselessly struck with emotional loss. Some of them are safely covered with headscarves, headbands, and hair grips – hazy eyes hanging between heavily mascara-lined lids, staring eerily into space behind black burkhas.

It is knowing that your own culture must be just as much of a shock to these others who look, speak and think so differently, too, that emphasises the reality of the circumstances. That although you feel that you are a good person, recruited to this country to assist in those charitable jobs and the helping-professions, you will be perceived as being different, strange, alien-like, non-understanding, and therefore, may easily be pushed aside.

A positive side

Luckily there is another side, too. Culture shock may carry with it the positive feeling of appreciation for what you have had and known, and that these things have helped to sculpture your life.

But together with that, it tells of a new time that has arisen, time to let go of your comfort zone, or at least part of it, and to embrace the differences that surround you.

You realize that you have to accept being part of another world, which may have no return to the known. Or perhaps returning to the once familiar, but this time in a changed and different way.

Of course the realisation that you are accepting your new cultural circumstances, which scream 'diversity,' will be shocking to your system. But if you allow it to happen, it will also contribute to the positive release of a new energy.

Energised by your new realisations, you will more readily be able to define your psychological standpoint at this moment in your life. Then you will be able to create a new, workable approach to building a new life and lifestyle in this new world of differences, which, simultaneously has strange similarities.

Eventually, these are all people who, just like you, have come to a country that in many ways is completely alien to them. They have experienced what you have experienced, and may still be going through.

Imagine having never seen and experienced anything other than a desert-like landscape, with people covered in Arabian-style clothes or wearing long white or black dresses with their faces covered in burkhas. Imagine being the child, or old person, coming from this background into a shockingly modern westernised city with its Western customs, clothes and temptations.

Or perhaps you are the Westerner moving to the Middle East or Far East, having taken up employment in Doha, Dubai, Tokyo, or Cairo.

No matter how big the differences are and how distanced you may feel from those around you, you are all created from the same energy; human beings with feelings, thoughts, dreams and a destiny beyond the place in which you live.

And like someone once said about our moral responsibility - it is not to stop the future, but to channel it in human directions. It is to ease the trauma of transition.

Chapter 11
Living is a mindset

Do you remember the time before you moved to your new country? How sure you were that you would succeed in both your personal and working life? How confident you were of your inner strengths, the quality of your level of perseverance, and the goal you had in mind?

The fact that many things have changed since then, just as much in your surroundings as within you, may be and should be something to be proud of at this stage. Simply because you know that you have dealt with a wide variety of personal, work, and other life issues as they have arisen, one by one, and on your own.

You will also realize that you have matured on many different levels, and that you have developed a much more integrated mindset. The latter is a fascinating product of integrated qualities through which you have learned that, in order to be able to cope in your personal and professional life, you must use the different forms of intelligence that are embedded in your creative mind.

This stretches beyond basic brain mechanics, as your emotional, social and spiritual mind becomes prominent, fuelled by the way in which you will be managing this mind of yours, or more straightforwardly: by 'running your brain', as Michael Hall and Bob Bodenhamer, experts in Neuro-Linguistic Programming, would call it.[48]

Managing your brain successfully depends on the qualities of your particular mind. These do not just jump forth as innate qualities, ready to be applied as situations arise. The basic energy and desire may be there, but you need to develop these qualities consciously and purposefully. This does not only apply to living in another country, it is something that should become part of your existence anyway – no matter where and who you are.

The Mind

We know that the human mind has developed remarkably from its primitive state to what it is today. Where the primitive mind harbours and marvels in uncontrolled emotions linked to basic instincts to ensure survival, the developed human mind today relies heavily on its cognitive structures and functioning: the conscious mind.

However, the unconscious mind holds the key to the way you are living your life, to your motivation to actively conquer your dreams in the country in which you have elected to resettle. It is in your unconscious mind that your strengths are embedded. From here, you can determine the direction for your life, and it is into that direction that you steer your life, from deep within.

The interaction between your conscious and unconscious mind therefore becomes a phenomenal playground where you will use your thoughts, not only in order to survive emotionally, but in terms of your complete psychological adjustment.

How you manage your brain, or the power of your mind, will eventually determine your success in your new world. Managing your brain is not a philosophical departure, but a realistic, basic way of living, essential if you have left your country and try to settle somewhere abroad.

What then do you exactly need to be able to make it in the new country?

Making it

The people making it are those who are strong inside and sure of what they want from life. They are focused and emotionally mature.

They know there will be difficulties and they accept that these exist. They avoid being overpowered by difficulties, instead facing these objectively and assess its possible impact on them and on their families.

Staying aware of their inner language and inner drive, they will also be the ones strong enough to recognize those cues within themselves indicating when to return to their home country would be the better option.

These kinds of people measure their success against their own standards, values and experiences, not those of others. They also realize that due to the changed circumstances brought about by their emigration, their beliefs often have to change. They consider that although this may impact on their values, it does not mean their morals must be abandoned. They therefore feel safe enough to start making some changes.

Above all, they have learnt that it is important to recognize when there are further smaller changes to make within the Big Change they had already made.

They explore the consequences of these new changes and know when to commence the new ones. Bridges firmly makes the point that you have to draw a line behind the past, accept that it is the past and that it is over, and commence with the new.[49] Those who know it and accept the challenge, indeed do just this.

This does not mean that you should abandon your past. You should rather take from it what is good and positive, those highlights in your developmental journey, and draw on these. Take what you have learned with you into your future and apply that which is applicable in your new circumstances.

Those who have made it work for them, are the ones who realize and recognize that there are certain mental processes which affect their adaptation to the new, and that these mental processes directly impact on the level of success that they eventually will achieve.

They accept that it happens on both a cognitive and emotional level, and they allow themselves to fully embark on these intertwined roads of change.

They acknowledge the strengths of their emotions, and manage these, rather than deny them. In fact, they try to make sense out of their emotions in an ongoing way and continuously find ways to use these effectively and productively.

They stay attentive to their family members' emotions and are willing to compromise when necessary without letting their focus go. They stick to realistic thinking. They consider their family. They continue to love.

Realistic thinking

In any form of thinking, there are certain cognitive processes involved alongside the emotional ones. During times of transitional change, these cognitive processes are usually strongly influenced by emotional thinking due to the reasons we have mentioned and discussed earlier.

It is especially then, during the emotional upheavals, that you therefore need to stick strongly to realistic thinking, and simultaneously stay aware of the dangers of regressing towards rigidity and of becoming inattentive to your inner self.

Goal-setting

You must keep your eye on your end goal, and if you do not have one, you should seriously consider where you are heading. Without specified direction and clearly defined goals, you will find it difficult to avoid plodding along or hitting pitfalls of emotional (and financial) disaster – like the painful position in the bottom of the U-curve where hopelessness and despair prevail.

A helpful exercise is to write down these goals. By formulating these very specifically, you will be able to evaluate if they are realistic and achievable. Review them regularly and adjust or change them when and where necessary. If you are sure about these, stick to them and work your way towards that end goal.

Success

It is important to define what success really means to you. How can you work towards something if you do not have a clear definition and image of it in your mind? In working purposely towards your goal whilst applying scrupulously the qualities of your emotional intelligence, you will get through those motions that perhaps, right at the beginning, were holding you back. You also should redefine your idea of success as time goes by. Circumstances change, and you should be able to adjust on an ongoing basis.

This may be a very stressful experience as time goes on and you therefore have to consider how you define success for yourself. Are the social and corporate ladders the only meaningful ones in this world? What about family and relationships? How do your changed values serve these? And how do they serve your own emotional and spiritual growth?

Consciously and unconsciously

To be specific about your goals and how to reach them, also means allowing your unconscious mind to direct you. Be aware of your unconscious mind, listen to what it is saying to you, talk to it, and accept its guidance.

Your unconscious is immensely powerful because it does not easily allow itself to be messed with. It has character, which has been carved with the blade of life itself by life itself, right across your years of existence.

The images are usually carved in strong lines while your mind tends to change them into movies, often subjective movies and therefore immensely powerful movies. These would direct the way you lead your life, direct the choices you make and direct the goals that you set for yourself.

The conscious mind on the other hand does not necessarily store all the information coming in. It sifts and weighs what is worthy and necessary to remember at that time, and considers what needs to be addressed there and then.

The rest of it does not just disappear. Hundreds of thousands of other stimuli have also entered your mind at that time; your conscience will suppress much of this information to your unconscious mind, where it will lie dormant until needed or until you are ready to confront it.

It will come to the conscious mind when something in your real world occurs, something about which the unconscious has felt very strongly. It will then trigger a response fuelled by the unconscious. This is usually a feeling, awareness or eventually a form of behaviour, which you may not necessarily have expected.

Your personal truth

We previously touched on personal truth. This time we are looking at it in more depth in order to understand the major role that it plays in your decisions and future planning. This truth is directly linked to your beliefs, and your spiritual intelligence.

Your beliefs, many of which date from your very early years, will tint your perception of the world around you. Your reactions are influenced by the meaning that you attach to something, and this meaning in turn, relates directly to your values.

Your personal truth is, therefore, a highly subjectively loaded pulpit from where you peer down and judge your outside world. Others may differ from it, in turn judge you for it, but they cannot say that it is wrong, because to you it is true and real. It is your reality.

In this sense, you can also say that it refers to the map of the world that you have drawn in your mind, your subjective world that indeed does not reflect reality.

With this in mind, conflict in your new work place, social surroundings and work life as well as within your family, could easily escalate within the stressful circumstances of adapting to the new. However, should you succeed in keeping in mind that everybody has his own truth, just like you, conflict will be dealt with more easily without you having to feel a victim of your circumstances.

Because you are not a victim.

Accepting responsibility

You have chosen this destination and moving here was an informed decision. Therefore you are responsible for the choices you made initially, and for the consequences of those choices that have followed since leaving your country. See to it that you are well informed about what you could expect in the new country – before you uproot. Be patient with this part of the emigration process, as it is the fundamental starting point.

The results of a research project on the psychological adjustment of students in foreign countries show that students who were informed about the country beforehand adjusted more easily and with fewer negative psychological effects.[50]

You could experience the same, particularly if you have given enough importance and meaning to the fact that things will be very different, and keep in mind the fact that your ideas and preconceptions are not set in stone. Refraining from rigid opinions may help you in opening yourself up for new learning – essential in the new life.

When the day comes that you feel and realize that you have started to settle down physically and emotionally, you will sense that you have new energy lying ready to be transformed into something new – something positive and productive.

Beliefs

Identify your beliefs – those set and often rigid ideas in your mind about how things are and should be. Assess and evaluate them scrupulously and objectively. Do they still have a place in your new life? Are they not perhaps outdated for the situation, or perhaps not at all applicable to the present?

How can you change them? Who will be upset and how will it upset them if you do? Could you communicate your reality to these people and help them to come to terms with the necessary changes that you have to make, not forgetting those that they might have to make? If the person is your partner, or child, or other significant figure in your life, can you maintain your relationship despite changing certain beliefs?

194

Do you really want to change your beliefs? Can you identify specific ways in which you will make your changes?

By letting go of old beliefs, you will open yourself up to new ones. These will increasingly play productive roles in developing your new life. For this to happen, you have to allow these new ideas to enter and to penetrate your mind, allowing your mind to assess them and to adopt them, and to integrate them into your everyday thinking.

It does not mean changing your morals. To acknowledge the rights of others, to respect others and to be a positive asset to your new surroundings, your pro-social morals should stay intact.

Relationships

Maintaining the good quality of your relationships will be crucial to you, now more than ever and therefore you need to be scrupulously honest with yourself and with your loved ones. Honesty does not have to be painful. Taking responsibility for honest communication is a crucial asset in your emotional and mental armoury.

If you notice communication start to suffer, seek professional guidance in dealing with the issues underlying this problem. It may be that you have some difficulties to accept change. Should you continue having problems in communicating in an honest and open way, this problem may directly impact on your re-settling, and could affect your emotional stability as well as that of your loved ones.

Fear and ego

Letting go can be a fearful experience, and so can your fears about your new life. To say the least, it is a real and haunting experience. Despite this threat, you can address your fears successfully. Fears are born and kept in the ego – that part of your mind which wants what it wants, when it wants. The ego is afraid of failure, of losing, of competition. It can easily manoeuvre and manipulate the conscious into patterns of obsessive thinking that focus mainly on gratification of the ego's needs.

The ego has no place in the success of meaningful living. Was it not living that you initially had in mind for you and your family? Was it not living in abundance that you wanted when trying to settle in? To be happy and content with your decisions and their outcomes, to be fulfilled as a human being who contributes positively to the wellbeing of others and to your loved ones?

If you are only driven by the desire and drive to become the best of all egos, the great achiever in the new country, you may soon become disillusioned and even thwarted.

The competition you will be facing is hard and omnipresent, as egos are all-over and involved in fierce workplace fighting. Once you set foot on this path, you could become absorbed in its fast-flowing river, which might drown you spiritually and push you out relentlessly.

Of course, you have to put in a lot of energy in order to stay focused on your goal and thereby to achieve the position you have planned for. This is good, but to stumble and push towards it using others as stepping-stones, including your family, only for egoistic gratification, may eventually leave you outside in the cold.

Should you suddenly comprehend the fact that your fears and anxieties are unrealistic and have become outdated and out of place, and see how they affect the quality of your work, social and emotional life, then face the situation and address it.

If you do not address these fears and anxieties, they can become instrumental in the way that you function. You would then send out a message of non-coping.

Before long, you could be in the vicious cycle of an enduring pattern of self-defeating behaviour. To change such behaviour would require intense self-exploration and emotional input, as well as decisive action in order to conquer its destructiveness, requiring loads of emotional energy, which you otherwise could have invested into your socio-psychological, spiritual, mental and professional growth and development.

Accountable decision-making

We previously have learnt about Sarah, whose thoughts have become a cycle of emotional turmoil leading from one negative thought to the next, feeding her brain with an ongoing pattern of negative thinking. This has caused her in the end to enter the downward spiral, maintaining a well-trodden route through the valleys of low self-esteem, low energy and discriminative but emotionally distorted thinking, right through long distances of psychological tunnel-vision.

In order to avoid these types of dangerous pitfalls, you should continue to stay alert by actively sidestepping any possible tendencies of similar self-defeating behaviour. Avoid becoming trapped in your own mind. Choose another route. The one leading to emotional freedom that enhances cognitive abilities, the ability to think clearly and to be able to honestly assess your situation and to adapt yourself to changed situations.

Responsible and accountable decisions ask for a clear mind. You owe this to your family, your work and above all to yourself.

Stay focused, live in the present.

Keep track and stay focused on a balanced life. If you have never had a balanced life before, now will be the time to seriously explore and invest in such. And live in the present.

To adjust successfully, and as quickly as possible, be yourself. Acknowledge your strengths out loud (for yourself) and do loads of positive self-talk. Talk to your partner too, test your opinions in this way, show appreciation for your partner's and your children's encouragement, especially when it comes non-verbally by way of gestures. They mean well. And do the same for them – make it a way of life.

Watch out!

In order to maintain your work permit, you must maintain your work. To maintain your work means to maintain high quality production.

However, be on the lookout for bullying at work. Some employers go out of their way to ask much more of their foreign recruits, knowing they will give and give because the recruits want their work-permits to be renewed at the end of the contract...

Ongoing training

Enrol for new qualifications from the new country. Do not worry if these appear to be of a lower standard than yours from home. Having a qualification with a logo from a local institution will speed you towards your career objectives. It also tells something about you; that you value what your new country offers and are willing to adapt to their requirements for success, whilst also showing that you appreciate their education system. Important!

Attend as many training events as possible in your workplace. This will be valued by your employer, who may see your enthusiasm as being ambitious, positive and forward-thinking. Do not fear to ask, and accept instructions and direction willingly and with good grace.

Consider continuing to develop your personal interests, in order to have something valuable at your command if you should ever return to your own country, or for when you retire.

Beware of becoming trapped on the ladders of organisational hierarchies, as these can lead to a cul-de-sac in many facets of your life; the consequences and pain can be serious once you realize that you have spent your entire life on a ladder which in actual fact is a lonely island in life's ocean.

The learning mind is the growing mind, if the mind keeps track of the heart. Isn't it?

Be an ambassador

Speak highly of your country of origin without lying and without pretending yours is better than theirs. Remember you are here now.

If you are confronted with sad and bad truths about your country (like in my case the sad history of South Africa's apartheid era) do not deny, minimise or rationalise, but focus on the here and now and highlight the positive developments that have taken place since.

Be an ambassador of your own country without boasting, without continuously comparing the old and the new country and definitely do not run down the new one. If there are real issues (which are most likely to be the case) and you cannot do something about it, keep it to your inner circle or private support system.

Build positive relationships

Build a positive relationship with your mentor or a line manager whom you can trust. Tactfully, let them understand your need for positive adjustment in the work and country and the attempts that you have been making in this regard, whilst maintaining your high work standards and ethics. If you have previously sensed that they did not fully trust you as a foreigner, assess this information – and show that you indeed are a trustworthy foreigner ready to embrace the new.

Also surround yourself with positive people – people who are goal-directed and motivated to make something of their lives in the new country, but who are also sensitively tuned to your needs and unique personality, without being patronizing or judgmental.

Their positive attitudes will have a positive ripple effect on you. Apply also your own talents, skills, understanding, empathy and humour to also enrich their lives. Nobody leaves anybody else without having been an influence of one kind or other. See that yours is positive and encouraging.

Develop networks for social support

Developing support systems is not only in the interest of your children, but also in yours and your spouse's or partner's. It will be meaningful for maintaining the health and well-being of your family and your marriage or relationship. In this way, you will prevent yourself from falling prey to a lonely, marginalised life apart from your community.

To be alone and lonely in a community is not always the other's fault; perhaps there is something within you that excludes others. Perhaps it has nothing to do with your host country and its people. Perhaps you are just not ready yet, as we have discussed in earlier chapters. You should address this soon so that you can experience the richness of community life – even if it is only that occasional social event.

Trust your creativity and reach out to those in your community who would gain by your social, emotional and professional skills. Perhaps you want to take the lead in making communities aware of the emotional and social needs of immigrants in their immediate communities. Perhaps you are the one who can change the negative stigma that the word "immigrant" has to some people and some communities by displaying your love and concern for others, including 'them'.

This is not something 'nice' to do. It is something that has become essential in our modern living within multi-racial and culturally diverse communities. We have to improve our understanding and acceptance of another, pro-actively and pro-socially. You have a role to play, too.

Change your inner language

Be realistic, and be positive. Consciously and purposefully focus on using more positive words, in writing, in talking quietly to yourself and in speaking generally, especially if your work entails depressive circumstances like in those of the medical, social work and probation service careers where words with negative connotations may sometimes be used.

If you have to write reports on psycho-social problems and criminal behavior as psychiatric nurses, social workers, police and probation officers often do, you may find that should you yourself have a dull or depressing lifestyle, you may easily become depressed within your new circumstances – especially if your working conditions are not what you had expected them to be. This can lead to serious stress-related problems within the workplace and could impact on your future working life.

Consider, then, establishing a new habit of writing for about fifteen minutes in the evening about something positive you have seen or experienced during the day – even the smallest thing. It could be the bus-trip back home after work, the funny guy standing in the queue, or the flowers in the park.

Write down your feelings and observations when it happened, and play the positive event over in your mind, enjoying the feelings that it recreates. It will help you to deal with stress more effectively and help you to stay more focused, as you consciously and purposely work towards restoring the balance.

Build and improve self-esteem

Make building your self-esteem, which may have undergone a bit of a knock during the first phases of the big change, a regular exercise. A good way of doing this is by associating with positive people who acknowledge your strengths and courage, but most of all, who accept you as the person who you are, even when you have your natural lows.

Just remember that you cannot always expect them to have a deep understanding of those losses that you have suffered. If they have not experienced the emotional impact of emigration and immigration issues, they would hardly understand. And do not bore them by becoming a nagging, moaning ex-pat.

Stay kind and polite towards the locals, even if some of them are the stiff upper-lip sort, and harness yourself against the unfriendliness and rejection of those locals who try to belittle you in their subtle and often direct ways. (They are not at all as many as you may think.)

Know that if you have not offended them, that it is not about you, it is most likely about you being a foreigner, an immigrant. You will not be the first person to have experienced this.

Believe

Believe in yourself. You have come a long way, longer and further than many others around you. Feel proud of yourself and give yourself credit. Look into your inner self and paint that beautiful picture in words – or even on a real canvas, with powerful music in the background.

Believe also in your family. They have been trying just as hard as you. Encourage them to join you in celebrating your family's success. Perhaps you want to make a collage, a painting, a sculpture. Make it a joyful family project, use loads of colour and like what you see. Talk about how you have developed and grown from the first day to now. And set new future goals for yourselves. We never stop developing.

Learn from the children

Learn from your children, who so often adjust so much quicker and easier, if their parents allow them to. Most of the people I have spoken to who emigrated to England during their childhood or teenage years, say they see England as their country and have no yearning to return to the land of their birth. They have settled as they have come to identify with the new country.

It was remarkable how many of them acknowledged and understood that their parents, especially their mothers, may have found it more difficult than them to work through this lengthy process. They did not hesitate to sympathise with their parents' sense of loss and adjustments in the process, although perhaps for some of the parents, it had not felt or looked like that.

The message that I got from most of them was one of admiration: admiring their parents for the big step that they had taken in order to provide to them, the children, a new life and new horizons.

There are however, also those children who found adjustment to the new extremely difficult, but tried to hide it from their parents. They felt that they had to live up to the expectation of the parents who had worked so hard to make it work in the new country.

As a responsible and emotionally intelligent parent you should stay alert to your children's deeper needs in terms of coming to terms with their changed circumstances, their grief, but also celebrate with them their new achievements and victory in their new life.

Victim or victor

Eventually there are two options: becoming victim or victor – victim of your emigration, or victor over your immigration. To remain the victor over your immigration means to be in touch with every part of your being, and to allow these parts to exist and to develop in equal measure. It is not only your cognitive and emotional mind that needs to develop and grow, but your spirituality, too.

Spiritual sensitivity

We have learnt that the spiritual mind keeps itself busy with the greater awareness of mental and spiritual completion. It contains a sense of greater wholeness. It is not only in your personal connection with God, or with that Greater or Higher Being or Energy, but it is also in your active seeking for the freedom and peace that unity brings along – oneness with and within the universe.

It contains the gift of forgiveness, as forgiveness commences within itself, within its sense of the need for togetherness and for emotional freedom. It bestows upon you the deep awareness of gratitude and thankfulness.

And you want to thank God for what He has provided you with: to be that person in that specific place in that specific country on that specific time. A person filled with those inner resources of resilience, perseverance and realistic optimism.

And love. Love for your country of origin, love for your people back home, love for your new country, for those around you now and above all – love for yourself and love for your God.

For every day is a new day. Hold on to its challenges and never fail to reach beyond its horizons. In the words of John F. Kennedy:

'We choose to go to the moon in this decade and do the other things, not because they are easy, but because they are hard, because that goal will serve to organize and measure the best of our energies and skills, because that challenge is one that we are willing to accept, one we are unwilling to postpone, and one which we intend to win, and the others, too.'

-end-

Appendix
Helpful hints once you are there

Complete this list as time moves on and keep it close-by:

(i) Register at your local authorities for a National Insurance Number (United Kingdom); or in other countries, find out upon arrival what you have to do and where you have to go to have this equivalent completed.

(ii) The Citizen's Advice Bureau (or equivalent in countries other than the UK) is a helpful contact for a list of enquiries that you may have.

(iii) Find the address and telephone number of your country's Embassy and Consulate (the latter deals with passports and registrations and the former with administrative functions).

(iv) Do not terminate medical and other insurance policies that you hold in your home country. You never know.

(v) Keep the telephone number of your children's new school at hand and look for a trustworthy person to act as a contact person in case you're not available. (Better still: Leave everything and see to your children's needs immediately in case of emergencies, especially in the beginning. Your employer should understand this.)

(vi) Register at a dentist's and general practitioner's practice in your area.

(vii) Master the transport system of your new country. The sooner you do so, the sooner you will feel more in control and confident. This would not only save you loads of stress and fuel, but you will be fighting global warming too!

(viii) Find places that sell your home country's food and treat your-self to it once in a while. The internet is a great source of information.

(ix) Look up and join your local community's social places. A local church with doctrines similar to yours is a helpful start.

(x) Find out if your own church has an international ministry with a church in your own language somewhere near you. Go there if you have the need, but also involve yourself in your local community's church, if it is in line with your beliefs.

(xi) Get to know a nearby neighbour. Do not wait for them to make the first contact. Do not expect that being neighbours automatically means being friends.

(xii) Compile a file with guidelines and instructions on what to do if a family crisis would strike. Discuss it with your family. Let a confidant in the new country, your people back home and your children have access to it.

(xiii) Keep crisis-money available and accessible for unforeseen emergencies, also for.those circumstances you do not want to think about: return flights, death, disasters.

(xiv) Learn the language and speak it with confidence. Your accent is only one of many.

(xv) Enjoy your new surroundings.

(xvi) Maintain a healthy lifestyle: physically and mentally.

(xvii) Do not burn your bridges. Stay in contact.

(xviii) Value your relationships, value your life.

(xix) Give thanks to God. He loves you and knows your needs and joy, wherever you will be.

(xx)   Add your own list of contacts, telephone numbers and hints and review them regularly:

....
....
....
....
....
....
....
....
....
....
....
....
....
....
....
....
....
....
....
....
....
....
....
....
....
....
....
....
....
....

-end-

Acknowledgements

My most sincere gratitude goes to everybody who made this book possible. Thank you to everyone who so willingly shared with me their innermost experiences. It is for reasons of confidentiality and to protect their privacy that I do not mention their names.

Thank you to those who spent time to read my drafts and who provided me with excellent advice. A special thanks to my South African nephew and friend, Dr. Heinz Meier, who used some precious holiday time in England to do so; and also to my British-South African friend and confidant, Sonja de Goede. Your honesty is much appreciated.

I thank all of those leaders and elders who have crossed my path; who over many years shaped me with their valuable and rich experiences. For the late Dr. Norman Cliff and his wife Joyce, and my first British neighbour Barbara Gatherum, who continued to inspire me silently with their love and support. Also my parents – thank you for introducing me to the wonder of learning and exploring, and for your loving support through the years.

My appreciation goes especially to my husband, Jac, and our daughter, Tanya, who patiently witnessed and allowed me my own ebb and flow, who continued to believe in me and who supported me unconditionally in my dedication to this research and writing. I admire their strength, perseverance and determination over the years – they have inspired and empowered me more than they will ever realize.

To our family and friends back home in South Africa, especially my parents, our siblings, Jac's children and grand-children:

To them I shall always be indebted – that they could let go because they believe that what we have is more than thousands of miles.

Endnotes

References

1 Bridges, William (1995)
2 Encarta dictionary
3 Bridges, William (1995)
4 Proshaska, James, O and Norcross, John. C (1994)
5 Shaffer, David, R. (1985)
6 Legrain, Philippe (2006)
7 Holmes, Holmes and Rahe http://medical- dictionary.the-freedictionary.com
8 Carlson, Neil R (1995)
9 Carlson, Neil R (1995)
10 Carlson, Neil R (1995)
11 Goleman, Daniel (1996)
12 Hall, Michael and Bodenhamer, Bob (2003)
13 Carlson, Neil, R (1995)
14 Bridges, William (1995)
15 http://blog.taragana.com/politics/2010/05/01/criteria-for-diagnosis-of-ptsd-changing-rapidly-32496
16 http://mighealth.net/uk/index.php/Refugees_and_asylum_seekers_-_State_of_Health
17 Bridges, William (1995)
18 Worden, William, J (1995)
19 Parkes, Colin Murray (1998)
20 Kübler-Ross, Elisabeth and Kessler, David (2005)
21 Williams, Dai http://www.eoslifework.co.uk/transmgt1.htm
22 Worden, William, J. (1995)

23 Sue,David, Sue, Derald & Sue, Stanley (1991)

24 Kübler-Ross, Elisabeth and Kessler, David (2005)

25 Legrain, Philippe (2006)

26 In Shaffer , David, R. (1985)

27 Chin-ning Chu (1995)

28 Baron, Robert and Byrne, Donn (1997)

29 Mayer, F, Stephan & Sutton, Karen (1996)

30 Morrison,Val & Bennett, Paul. (2006)

31 Mills, Harry and Dombeck, Mark http://www.mentalhelp.net/poc/view_doc.php

32 Mayer, F., Stephan & Sutton, Karen (1996)

33 Mayer, F., Stephan & Sutton, Karen (1996)

34 Ogden, Jane (2005)

35 Kiyosaki, Robert, T. (2004)

36 Damasio, Antonio (2000)

37 Feltham, Colin and Horton, Ian (2000)

38 Feltham, Colin and Horton Ian (2000)

39 Bridges, William (1995)

40 Goleman, Daniel (2006)

41 Goleman, Daniel (2007)

42 Internet Royal College of Psychiatrists

43 Internet Royal College of Psychiatrist

44 (http://www.abundanceinmylife.com/spirituality4.html

45 Legrain, Philippe (2006)

46 Sue, David, Sue, Derald & Sue, Stanley (1994)

47 Williams, Dai http://www.eoslifework.co.uk/transmgt1.htm

48 Hall, Michael and Bodenhamer, Bob (2004)

49 Bridges, William (1995)

50 Internet Nurses College research

Bibliography
And Recommended Reading

ADLER, HARRY & HEATHER, BERYL. (1999) *NLP in 21 Days. A complete Introduction and Training Programme.* London: Judy Piatkus (Publishers) Limited

ANDREAS, STEVE & FAULKNER, CHARLES (2003) *NLP. The New Technology of Achievement.* London: Nicholas Brealey Publishing

BARON, ROBERT, A. & BYRNE, DONN (1997) Social *Psychology. Understanding Human Interaction.* (7th Edition). London: Allyn and Bacon

BARLOW, David, H and DURAND, Mark (1995) *Abnormal Psychology.* London: Brooks/Cole Publishing Company.

BRIDGES, WILLIAM (1995) Managing *Transitions: .Making the Most of Change.* London: Nicholas Brealy Publishing Limited

CARLSON, NEIL, R. (1995) *Foundations of Physiological Psychology.* (3rd Edition) London: Allan and Bacon

CHU, CHIN-NING (1995) *Thick Face, Black Heart. The Asian Path to Thriving, Winning and Succeeding.* London: Nicholas Brealey Publishing.

COVEY, STEPHAN (1994) *The Seven Habits of Highly Successful People. Powerful Lessons in Personal Change.* London: Simon and Schuster Limited.

DAMASIO, ANTONIO. (2000) *The feeling of what happens: body, emotion and the making of consciousness.* London: Vintage

DYER, WAYNE, W. (2008) The *Power of Intention. Change the way you look at things and the things you look at will change.* London: Hay House UK Limited

ENCARTA ® WORLD ENGLISH DICTIONARY

FELTHAM, COLIN & HORTON, IAN (2000) Handbook *of Counselling and Psychotherapy.* London: Sage Publications

FENNELL, MELANIE (1999) *Overcoming Low Self-Esteem. A self-help guide using Cognitive Behavioral Techniques.* London: Constable & Robinson Ltd

FORGAS, JOSEPH, P. (2001) *Feeling and Thinking. The Role of Affect in Social Cognition.* Cambridge: Cambridge University Press

GOLEMAN, DANIEL (1998) *Working with Emotional Intelligence.* London: Bloomsbury Publishing Plc.

GOLEMAN, DANIEL (1996) Emotional *Intelligence. Why it can matter more than IQ.* London: Bloomsbury Publishing Plc.

GOLEMAN, DANIEL (2007) *Social Intelligence. The New Science of Human Relationships.* London: Arrow Books

GOLEMAN, DANIEL (2003) The *New Leaders.* London: Bloomsbury Publishing Plc.

GILBERT, PAUL. (2000) *Overcoming Depression. A self-help guide using Cognitive Behavioral Techniques.* London: Robinson Publishing Limited.

HALL, L. MICHAEL & BODENHAMER, BOB, G. (2004) *The User's Manuel for the Brain. The Complete Manuel for Neuro-Linguistic Programming Practitioner Certification.* Vol I. Camarthen, Wales: Crown House Publishing Limited.

HALL, L. MICHAEL & BODENHAMER, BOB, G (2003) *The User's Manuel for the Brain. The Complete Manuel for Neuro-Linguistic Programming. Mastering Systemic NLP. Vol II.* Camarthen, Wales: Crown House Publishing Limited

HAWTON, KEITH, SALKOVSKIS, PAUL, M KIRK, JOAN & CLARK, DAVID M. (2001) *Cognitive Behaviour Therapy for Psychiatric Problems. A Practical Guide.* Oxford: Oxford University Press.

HOWARD, CHRISTOPHER. (2004) *Turning Passions into Profits. 3 Steps to Wealth and Power.* New Jersey: John Wiley & Sons, Inc.

KIYOSAKI, Robert T. (2004) *Rich Dad, Poor Dad. What the rich teach their kids – that you can learn too.* London: Time Warner Book Group.

KÜBLER-ROSS, ELISABETH AND KIESLER, DAVID. (2005) *On Grief and Grieving. Finding the Meaning of Grief Through the Five Stages of Loss.* London: Simon & Schuster Inc.

KNIGHT, SUE (1995) *NLP at Work. Neuro-Linguistic Programming. The difference that makes a difference in business.* London: Nicholas Brealy Publishing Ltd.

LEGRAIN, PHILIPPE (2006) *Immigrants. Your country needs them.* London: Little, Brown.

MADDI, Salvatore, R. (1996) *Personality Theories. A Comparative Analysis.* 6th Edition. London: Brooks/Cole Publishing Company

MAYER, F, STEPHAN & SUTTON, KAREN (1996) *Personality: An Integrative Approach.* New Jersey: Prentice-Hall

MORRISON, VAL & BENNETT, PAUL (2006) *An Introduction to Health Psychology.* London: Prentice-Hall

OGDEN, JANE (2005) Health *Psychology. A Textbook.* (3rd Edition) Maidenhead, Open University Press

PARKES, COLIN MURRAY (1998) *Bereavement. Studies of Grief in Adult Life.* London: Penguin

PEARSALL, JUDY (2001) *Oxford Dictionary.* 10th Edition. Oxford University Press.

PROCHASKA, JAMES, O. & NORCROSS, JOHN, C. (1994) *Systems of Psychotherapy. A Trans-theoretical Analysis.* 3rd Edition. London: Brooks/Cole Publishing Company

SCHAFFER, DAVID R (1985) *Developmental Psychology. Childhood and Adolescence.* (4th Edition) London: Brooks/Cole Publishing

SUE, DAVID, SUE, DERALD & SUE, STANLEY (1994) Understanding *Abnormal Behavior.* 4th Edition.   Boston: Houghton Mifflin Company

WORDEN, J. WILLIAM   (1995) *Grief Counselling   and Grief Therapy. A Handbook for the Mental Health Practitioner.* London: Routledge

Other Sources

Monash Institute, London: Symposium on South Africans in Britain June 2008

BBC news article : Breakfast show (2008/05/05)

Internet: Home Office UK

Internet Royal college of psychiatrists

http://www.rcpsych.ac.uk/mentalhealthinfo/treatments/spirituality. aspx

(http://www.jfklibrary.org/Historical+Resources/ Archives/Reference+Desk/Speehes/ JFK/003POF03SpaceEffort09121962.htm)

http://www.eoslifework.co.uk/transmgt1.htm

http://blog.taragana.com/politics/2010/05/01/criteria-for-diagnosis-of-ptsd-changing-rapidly-32496

http://mighealth.net/uk/index.php/Refugees_and_asylum_ seekers_-_State_of_Health

About The Author

Being a social worker, psychotherapist and counselor, *Christa de Vries* practices as a Masters NLP practitioner in stress and change management, hypnotherapy, and psychological therapy and counseling.

In addition to her clinical practice she has extensive experience as social worker in both forensic and other socio-psychological assessment and therapeutic work, as well as in consultancy, whilst also having previously worked as expert witness in family, criminal and civil courts in South Africa. During recent years she has added to her professional and cultural repertoire as assessor and professional report-writer in England's Criminal Justice System.

'Working with people from all walks of life during times when they struggle emotionally in having to make life-changing decisions, or when change and transition have slowed down their usual pace and capacity to overcome barriers, have enriched my life enormously. To be able to bring to the fore others' hidden strengths, and to assist them in unleashing their potential to overcome obstacles blocking their mental and psychological growth, are of the most rewarding things to experience.'

Christa matriculated at the Hoërskool Vaalharts, Jan Kempdorp, South Africa in 1973. She since had obtained her undergraduate and post-graduate degrees in Social Work, Counseling and Psychology at the Universities of Pretoria, South Africa, and Johannesburg (RAU) in 1976, 1990 and 2000, respectively), with further studies in the UK.

CPSIA information can be obtained at www.ICGtesting.com
Printed in the USA
LVOW07s1903090215

426300LV00002B/652/P